MONEY TROUBLE

SURVIVING YOUR FINANCIAL CRISIS

MONEY TROUBLE

SURVIVING YOUR FINANCIAL CRISIS

DEBORAH MCNAUGHTON and MELINDA WEINSTEIN

BEACON HILL PRESS
OF KANSAS CITY

Copyright 2009
by Deborah McNaughton and Melinda Weinstein and
Beacon Hill Press of Kansas City

ISBN 978-0-8341-2473-8

Printed in the
United States of America

Cover Design: J.R. Caines
Interior Design: Sharon Page

All Scripture quotations not otherwise designated are from the *Holy Bible, New International Version*® (niv®). Copyright © 1973, 1978, 1984 by International Bible Society. Used by permission of Zondervan Publishing House. All rights reserved.

Permission to quote from the following additional copyrighted version of the Bible is acknowledged with appreciation:

The *New King James Version* (nkjv). Copyright © 1979, 1980, 1982 Thomas Nelson, Inc.

Library of Congress Cataloging-in-Publication Data

McNaughton, Deborah, 1950-
  Money trouble : surviving your financial crisis / Deborah McNaughton and Melinda Weinstein.
    p. cm.
  ISBN 978-0-8341-2473-8 (pbk.)
  1. Finance, Personal—Religious aspects. 2. Finance, Personal—United States. I. Weinstein, Melinda. II. Title.
  HG179.M2513 2009
  332.024—dc22

2009019664

This publication is designed to provide accurate and authoritative information. It is sold with the understanding that the publisher and authors are not engaged herein in rendering legal, accounting, or other professional services. If legal advice or other expert assistance is required, the services of a competent professioinal should be sought.

10 9 8 7 6 5 4 3 2 1

CONTENTS

Preface	7
1. Are You Drowning in Debt?	13
2. When the Going Gets Tough: Dealing with Stress	25
3. Figure Out How You Blew It	35
4. Symptoms of Too Much Debt	43
5. Talk About It	55
6. Dealing with Collectors: Hiding Won't Help	67
7. Problem Home Loans	81
8. Avoiding Foreclosure	89
9. Alternatives to Bankruptcy, Eviction, Lawsuits or Repossession	99
10. Communicate Successfully with Creditors	109
11. Payment Priorities: Dealing with Stress During a Financial Crisis	121
12. Budget Strategies That Work	135
13. Plug the Cash Leak, and Increase the Cash Flow	151
14. Get Out and Stay Out—of Debt	165
15. Protect Yourself from Identity Theft	181
16. Build Your Credit Report	191
17. Money Miracles	205
18. Financial Victory	213
Additional Resources	219
About the Authors	222

PREFACE

> Then you will call, and the Lord will answer;
> you will cry for help, and he will say: Here am I.
> —Isaiah 58:9

Isaiah 58:9 saved my sanity. It gave me hope. It gave me strength and comfort from God as we faced one of our darkest times during a financial crisis. My cry was *Where are you, God? I can't make it one more day!* As I paced and cried, God showed me this scripture, and it turned my world around. He let me know that things would be all right.

I learned about finances the hard way—by living with the consequences of unwise financial decisions. Why is it that we often must learn things the hard way before we start making changes? Is it human nature? Or is it thinking that things will be better when a good break comes our way?

I was never taught the proper way to manage money. My husband and I owned a real estate franchise business in the 1980s. We had good years and bad years. The real estate business was always feast or famine, with the deciding factor being how the economy was going.

As our business grew, I recognized the need to help some of our potential clients get their credit and spending under control in order to qualify for a loan to purchase a home. I researched several laws pertaining to credit restoration, and as a result I founded Professional Credit Counselors. My main intention was not only to help people with their credit needs but also to add to our real estate business. I had head knowledge and empathy and a desire to help people.

I certainly never expected that one day I would be nearly bankrupt.

I know from experience that owning a business can sometimes create a false sense of security. There was always that potential big deal just ahead that was going to make all my financial dreams come true. No need to worry about tomorrow with that big deal so close!

I have news for you: the big deal rarely happens. Proverbs 21:5 says, "The plans of the diligent lead to profit as surely as haste leads to poverty." There really are no reliable get-rich-quick schemes. If that big deal is around the corner, it will be icing on the cake, not something you can count on to bail you out of debt and solve all your money woes.

In the early 1990s my husband and I decided to sell our real estate franchise and invest the money in another business. The new business never got off the ground. The country was in an economic downturn, and we were caught in it. The money we had invested was gone, resulting in a seventy-percent drop in our income.

We had been living quite well, never planning on a business failure. The money we had saved was not enough to keep us going for very long, and what little we had was quickly used up as we tried to keep the creditors happy. The bill collectors weren't interested in hearing about the loss of income—they just wanted their money. The bills just kept coming.

Most of the debt was from business loans, a few credit cards, and taxes. Including late fees and penalties, the total we owed was more than $300,000—and compounding.

The stress was awful; there was no peace. Bill collectors had no sympathy and called us day and night demanding money. Sleepless nights were frequent.

Bankruptcy wasn't an option. The taxes we owed couldn't be discharged anyway, and we didn't want to jeopardize the family partnership.

I knew how to deal with creditors, but I didn't have the money to pay them. Decisions had to be made on what bills we could pay and how we were going to take care of our family.

PREFACE

This was not an overnight problem; the events I describe here went on for several years. The hole we were in was very deep, and it was going to take quite a while to get out of it.

As we began to dig our way out of the pit, we made some bad decisions, and we listened to some bad advice. The Bible says, "Listen to advice and accept instruction, and in the end you will be wise" (Proverbs 19:20). We listened to advisers, and even though my husband, Hal, and I felt uneasy, we followed their advice anyway. Later we realized that the uneasiness was from God, and we should have followed our instincts. If we had, most of our financial problems could have been avoided. We know now that we should have sought counsel from more than one adviser, but we didn't. In our stressed-out, desperate situation, we found it difficult to know right from wrong.

Once the dust settled, we finally developed a plan and a budget that would help us dig out while meeting our family's needs.

When reviewing ways to save money and cut back on some of our expenses, I decided to quit paying the premium for our medical insurance. I planned to pick it up later when things weren't so tight. Besides, we were all healthy.

Thirty days after letting our medical insurance lapse, my youngest daughter, Melinda, underwent emergency brain surgery. What appeared as flu-like symptoms turned out to be hydrocephalus, a blockage in the ventricles of her brain that caused a build-up of fluid, resulting in a coma and near death. A neurosurgeon was brought in, and she was rushed into surgery. Her life was at stake, and we didn't know what her condition would be if she survived. And we had no medical insurance.

I was so afraid my daughter would die and was deeply concerned that when the hospital found out we had no medical insurance they would not give her the care she needed. Bankruptcy seemed inevitable.

But thanks be to God, Melinda's surgery was a success, and she suffered no side effects. We are a praying family, and there was also a prayer chain of people praying for Melinda all across the United States.

More good news was that the hospital had a special program for children with traumas, and Melinda fit the profile. That program paid for all medical expenses over $50,000. Even knowing we had no insurance, the hospital personnel brought in the best specialists and medical team to help save my daughter's life.

A week after Melinda's health crisis, our family was emotionally drained. To make matters worse, the Internal Revenue Service (IRS) had taken what little money we did have in our bank account during the week of Melinda's surgery. I had made a verbal pay arrangement with the IRS but had failed to get it in writing.

When I called the IRS, I was emotional as I described all that we had been through during Melinda's illness and surgery. After realizing there had been a miscommunication, the lady I spoke with returned the money the IRS had taken except for $100, and a new pay arrangement was made.

This chain of events changed my life and the life of my family. We made career changes, because we knew we would need medical insurance for Melinda, and she now had a preexisting condition.

Just as you may be today, we were caught in a web created by a poor economy and our own poor decisions, but we bounced back. We reevaluated our priorities and steadfastly made the necessary changes.

Were we able to pay back the $300,000? No. But we negotiated with each of our creditors, and they accepted less. Our creditors didn't want us to file for bankruptcy, because they would end up getting nothing, and we wanted to handle our obligations as honorably as we possibly could. Something was better than nothing in their opinions, and we were able to avoid bankruptcy. The process took several years, because we did not make an offer to a creditor unless we had the money in hand to pay what we agreed to pay.

It has now been many years since our personal journey through those financial hardships. Our daughters are now married and have children of their own. But our experience created in me a passion to help educate people on the right way to handle their finances so they can avoid the trauma my family and I went through.

As a matter of fact, Melinda began working with me in 2001. Together we founded Financial Victory Institute, through which we have educated and counseled thousands of people.

When I talk to clients or do interviews on radio or television, I can say honestly that I am a better person for having faced that trial. I remember asking God to allow at least one person's life to be changed by what I learned. The head knowledge I had regarding credit and debt is now teamed with the compassion I feel for those who are facing financial challenges. It is my desire to help restore and encourage them. I know what they're feeling—I've been there.

I trust that you, too, will be able to minister to others because of the lessons you will learn from the challenges you face. Because of our past, Melinda and I view our business as a ministry.

We have tried to make this book a user-friendly tool you can use to help you overcome your challenges and get a handle on your finances. We have included worksheets you can use to get the full picture of your financial situation and develop a plan to overcome your money trouble.

Discouraging and frustrating days may loom ahead, but don't allow that to overwhelm you. I encourage you to pick yourself up, say a prayer, make a plan, get the help or advice you need, resolve to make wise and godly decisions, and keep moving forward. You can survive this crisis and find victory in your finances. It won't be accomplished overnight, but you can do it.

The scripture that took me to a new level of hope the day I cried out to God was Isaiah 58:11: "The LORD will guide you always; he will satisfy your needs in a sun-scorched land and will strengthen your frame. You will be like a well-watered garden, like a spring whose waters never fail."

Let's get started.

1
ARE YOU DROWNING IN DEBT?

> Do not be a man who strikes hands in pledge
> or puts up security for debts; if you lack the
> means to pay, your very bed will be
> snatched from under you.
> —Proverbs 22:26-27

Tears ran down Jane's face as she and her husband sat across from me. She had lost her job the previous day, and their world was turned upside down. They had bought two investment houses with plans to rent them out for one year and then sell them for profit. Instead, the market took a downturn, and the properties were worth less than they paid for them. Not only that, the mortgage payments were more than the rent they were receiving. Every extra penny they got their hands on had to go toward the payments on the rentals and the mortgage on their own home. They had used the equity in their home to buy the investment properties. Without Jane's income, they had no idea how they could make it.

* * *

Sarah called the office, frantic because she was behind on her bills. Collection agencies called her constantly. She could not sleep, and she was a nervous wreck. She wanted me to tell her what her options were.

* * *

Jack and Mary were in a state of gloom when they contacted our office. Their bills totaled more than their income, and they didn't know what to do. They fought regularly about money, and their marriage was suffering.

* * *

These are typical situations that credit counselors deal with.

Did God cause these problems? No. Then who is to blame? The first thing these folks and others must do is take *responsibility* for bad financial decisions they have made. The Bible warns us repeatedly to stay out of debt and to seek wise counsel. Psalms and Proverbs both contain many scriptures pertaining to money.

HOW DID I GET HERE?

Many people don't realize the importance of establishing credit and the responsibility of maintaining it. They see credit as a kind of blank check and don't keep track of what they're spending. Believing they can pay tomorrow for what they're enjoying today, they run up their debts. Before they know it, money trouble is looming.

No one sets out to get deeply into debt; it creeps up slowly. Most people are sincere in their intention to pay that credit card balance in full. The problem is that all those little purchases have added up to a balance that the budget can't support. Making only the minimum payment feels so much better.

High school doesn't teach it, college doesn't teach it, and parents rarely teach it: the importance and responsibility of using credit wisely. Those who reach adulthood with no education on managing money and debt are extremely vulnerable to financial disaster.

Frequently clients who come for credit consulting say to us, "If I had only known the importance of handling money, I would have done things differently."

Those who are prone to financial disaster usually have at least one of the following three personality traits: (1) eternal optimism, (2) believing in dreams, or (3) believing that things will get better if they just wait it out.

A person who has one or all of these personality traits runs an increased risk of succumbing to "big-deal-itis." People like this tend to live for the future and never face the present; they grab what they can right now without any concern for tomorrow, because the big deal is just around the corner. They live in perpetual denial.

These are the persons who have more bills to pay than money with which to pay them—you know, the ones who use credit cards as they would a blank check. Are you one of them?

Proverbs 16:20 says, "Whoever gives heed to instruction prospers, and blessed is he who trusts in the Lord." It is difficult to trust in the Lord when we're slaves to our wants and must-haves to satisfy the need for material things.

With no vision, no plan, no discipline or direction—and no one to come to your rescue—disaster just sits and waits.

A person without vision can't see what may be ahead and doesn't learn how the credit system works or how to manage debt. Once in debt, this person is left to wonder, *How did I get here?*

Without a plan to retire the debt you've incurred, you're stressed out and have difficulty sleeping. You feel overwhelmed. Prayer is absolutely essential, but it's important that you make a realistic plan tailored to your situation. We'll present several different strategies to help you formulate your plan.

No plan will work, though, if you don't exercise discipline. It's through planning *and* discipline that you'll achieve freedom from debt—and inner peace. You'll sense the yoke of bondage lifting from your shoulders as you take these first important steps.

You must have a financial roadmap to keep you moving in the right direction. In the following chapters we'll help you map your course from where you are right now to the end of your money trouble.

We know how upsetting and discouraging it is to feel that all is lost. Being overextended and drowning in debt, with bill collectors hounding you, makes you feel as if no one else has ever been in such a mess. Don't give in to discouragement—there's light at the end of the tunnel.

As the economy struggles, desperation rises; companies are closing their doors. At this writing, the real estate market is in decline, and people find themselves owing more on their homes than their homes are worth. With the uncertainty caused by declining markets, the rising cost of utilities and groceries, and the discouraging news of layoffs and cutbacks, many are trying to cut back on spending. Some have resorted to using credit cards and equity lines of credit to pay their bills. Renters are being pushed out of their homes because landlords can't afford the payments and the bank is foreclosing. Homeowners can't tap into their home equity because the banks have frozen lines of credit. Those with adjustable-rate mortgages face higher house payments.

With a downturn in the economy, many of us suddenly face a mountain of debt and no plan to conquer that mountain. Banks, department stores, and credit card companies love us when we pay on time; that love turns to aggressive collection tactics if we fall behind with payments.

Here's something to think about: If you hadn't borrowed and charged, would you be living without some of the luxuries you now enjoy? By "luxuries" we mean those things that can't really be classified as necessities: eating out, the to-die-for wardrobe, toys such as the big-screen television set and state-of-the-art computer, the latest and greatest gadgets for our children. Have these kinds of purchases led to excessive debt? Three little words open the door to the beginning of the end: *small monthly payment*.

Being knowledgeable about the use of credit and other financial matters empowers you to use self-control and avoid a financial crisis, whether it's here or is approaching.

ANNIE'S STORY

When we first met with Annie, she and her husband, Ben, were struggling to pay their bills. They had excessive debt, and two of their credit cards were delinquent. We instructed them to contact their creditors and make payment arrangements.

Several months later, Annie phoned us again to tell us that their situation had gotten worse. They had acquired $25,000 in credit card debt, and all their credit cards had become delinquent. They didn't own a home, so an equity loan wasn't a consideration. They had no assets.

Annie explained that both she and Ben were employed and also had a side business. Instead of paying their credit card bills, they were putting all extra money they had into the business. They were waiting for a "big deal" to come in so they could pay off their credit cards.

As soon as we heard about the "big-deal-itis," we knew they weren't living in the real world. This wasn't a new story to us. We had heard it over and over again from others who had gotten into side businesses or were self-employed and owned their businesses, to name just a few. As a matter of fact, we related to this because we had been down that road and quickly discovered that most big deals don't ever happen. As a matter of fact, if reality doesn't sink in really fast, people counting on a big deal to save them end up filing bankruptcy, which is exactly what Annie was considering.

Prayer works, but you also must get out of your comfort zone and take action. Your prayer should be for God to grant you knowledge and discipline to create a plan to help you overcome this financial crisis you face. Optimism is fine as long as you're also realistic in taking care of the immediate needs of your family and yourself.

Annie said that once the big deal came, they would pay off all their credit cards. But in the meantime she was having trouble dealing with the creditors who were calling and demanding payment.

We told Annie to not look at the big deal as their ticket to freedom but to look at it as icing on the cake. The proceeds of the big deal, if it materialized, should be added to what they are already doing financially and not be counted on as the only strategy for financial freedom. It was time for Annie and Ben to face reality and get their debt under control and their finances back on track.

We encouraged Annie to make a list of creditors and make payment arrangements with each of them. Since she and Ben were both employed, there were steady paychecks coming in to help them with their plan. It was also suggested that if they felt uncomfortable talking to each of the creditors themselves, they should contact a debt management company to assist them in working with their creditors.

If Annie and Ben's big deal does come in, they won't have to use every penny of it to catch up with bills. There will be enough to put away and save.

QUIZ TIME

Before you go any further, circle what you consider to be the correct answer to the following questions. Remember: knowledge is power, and this is knowledge that will help you get where you want to go.

1. When a credit card application arrives in the mail, before making a decision to apply, you
   a. Check the annual fees and other charges.
   b. Review the interest rates and the way the interest is calculated.
   c. Read the fine print.
   d. All of the above.
2. When a lender is deciding whether or not to approve your loan, what is the most important information the lender is seeking?
   a. Payment history from your credit report and income
   b. Number of dependents in the household and marital status
   c. Whether you rent or own your home
   d. An unlisted telephone number
3. When deciding whether to approve your credit application for a home, automobile, or credit card, the lender is looking for
   a. Your FICO score.
   b. Your debt-to-income ratio.
   c. Length of employment.
   d. All of the above.
4. When determining the cost of your loan, the most important indicator is
   a. Minimum monthly payment.
   b. Interest rate.
   c. Loan amount.

MONEY TROUBLE

   d. Number of monthly payments.
5. If you make a partial payment other than the amount due on your credit card statement, your credit report will reflect
   a. Delinquency.
   b. Payment is current.
   c. Unrated.
   d. None of the above.
6. If you have a credit card balance of $2,000, make the minimum payment each month, and never pay more than the minimum, how long will it take you to pay off this debt? (Your interest rate will be approximately 21 percent.)
   a. Two years
   b. Four years
   c. Eight years
   d. Sixteen or more years.
7. If you're self-employed, how many years will a creditor expect you to have been in business before granting credit?
   a. Two or more years
   b. Three or more years
   c. Four or more years
   d. Five or more years
8. Creditors see a red flag and your application is immediately denied if your debt-to-income ratio (excluding your mortgage or rent payments) is
   a. Two to seven percent of your take-home income.
   b. Eight to twelve percent of your take-home income.
   c. Twelve to nineteen percent of your take-home income.
   d. Twenty percent or higher of your take-home income.
9. When you get a credit card solicitation for a pre-approved card or application and don't want to apply for the card, you should
   a. Toss it into the trash.
   b. Shred or destroy the solicitation.
   c. Call the company and say that you decline the offer.

d. None of the above.
10. The ideal number of open accounts on your credit report should be
   a. Zero or one.
   b. Two or three.
   c. Four or five.
   d. Six or more.

REVIEW YOUR ANSWERS

1. **(d)** All of the above. When you receive a credit card application, read every word in the application and the disclosures. There may be fees charged such as an annual fee, over-the-limit fees, late fees, returned-check fees, and others. Also, know what the interest rate is and how interest is charged. There may be a grace period from the date of purchase (approximately twenty to twenty-five days) when no interest is charged. This grace period enables you to pay off the balance of new purchases without being assessed a finance charge. If there is no grace period, interest begins accruing at the time of purchase and is calculated daily.

2. **(a)** A lender will look at your credit report closely regarding your payment history. From the information taken from your credit report and your monthly income, the creditor will determine if you can likely make the payments on the credit you're applying for.

3. **(d)** The FICO score is a numeric tabulation of several factors listed on your credit report that include payment history, type of credit you currently carry, balances compared to credit limits, open accounts, and number of inquiries. FICO scoring is an important qualification when applying for credit. If you're overextended, your FICO score will be low. In addition to your FICO score, your debt-to-income is calculated to make sure you can handle the payments. If you've been employed for less than two years, you probably won't qualify for credit.

4. **(b)** Knowing how much interest you'll be paying is the most important factor in determining how much this loan or credit card is going to cost you. The higher the interest rate, the more you're paying in finance charges.
5. **(a)** If you're having trouble making your payment, a partial payment will be reported on your credit report as a delinquency. The difference in the payment made and the payment owed is rolled into the next month. This is called a "rolling late" and will not become current until the total payment is received. This is a negative mark on your credit report.
6. **(d)** If you make only the minimum payment on a credit card balance of $2,000, it will take sixteen years and eight months to pay it off. You'll also pay approximately $2,500 in interest.
7. **(a)** You must have been self-employed for two or more years to qualify for new credit. Financial statements such as tax returns, bank statements, and a year-to-date profit-and-loss statement may be required. A self-employed person is a higher risk for the lender, because the monthly income is not stable.
8. **(d)** Credit will be denied if your debt-to-income ratio is twenty percent or higher. Even fifteen percent and above would signal the lender that you may be headed for problems.
9. **(b)** If you get a credit card solicitation for a pre-approved card or application and don't want to apply for the card—shred it! Failing to do so leaves you open to identity theft.
10. **(b)** The ideal number of open accounts is two or three. You don't need more than that to show a payment pattern.

SCORING

9 to 10: Good job! You have good credit knowledge.

5 to 8: Be careful. Examine all solicitations and know what the contracts state. That means reading the fine print. Do your homework when applying for credit, and make sure you aren't going to be overextended and have more debt than you can afford.

0 to 4 correct: Watch out! Learn all you can about credit and debt. You could easily make a wrong decision that will result in excessive debt and financial problems.

TOUGH TIME TIPS

- Learn all you can about how the credit system works.
- Establish a plan to get out of debt.
- Be disciplined to avoid spending.

Knowledge is power in breaking free of debt and managing your finances.

2

WHEN THE GOING GETS TOUGH
DEALING WITH STRESS

God has not given us a spirit of fear,
but of power and of love and of a sound mind.
—2 Timothy 1:7, NKJV

Financial stress causes severe reactions of one type or another in almost everyone it touches—almost like an illness. When a person is ill, though, friends and family rally around to bring comfort—there's no embarrassment or shame.

When a person is going through a financial crisis, he or she sometimes turns to God for help—or blames God and walks away from Him. But God did not create the problem. Most financial disasters are caused from bad decisions and poor planning. When facing a financial problem, you may choose to isolate yourself from friends and loved ones rather than share with them what's happening in your life. You may feel alone—as if God has left you out there to fend for yourself. *The good news is that He has not.*

After the initial realization of the fix you're in and the first wave of self-pity is under control, you must become proactive in climbing out of this pit. Yes, there will no doubt be days when you don't feel like getting out of bed and anxiety will set in. But once you begin to proactively address the problem, you'll begin to feel better.

God will be faithful to take you by the hand and relieve your stress and fears. Proverbs 24:5-6 says "A wise man has great power, and a man of knowledge increases strength; for waging war you need guidance, and for victory many advisers." Becoming proactive during your financial crisis helps you stay focused on God rather than blame Him for your circumstances.

Every individual reacts differently when finances begin to crumble. Regardless of the severity of your situation, the most important thing you can do to facilitate your own recovery is to take responsibility and develop a plan. A financial crisis causes paralysis, stress, anxiety, and disorientation, because it becomes all you can think about.

Most of us have fears about money. It seems that no matter how hard we try, there's just never enough of it to go around, in good times or bad times. If you feel fearful and intimated by your financial situation, you're certainly not alone. Most people at some time in their lives will experience fear and anxiety about money matters. The best way to ease the stress is to learn and practice better money management for yourself and your family.

Money fears come in different shapes and sizes. Start a money journal, and write down what causes you the greatest stress and anxiety regarding your financial situation. Use the worksheet below.

Money Journal

List here what causes your greatest stress and anxiety regarding your finances.

_____
_____
_____
_____
_____
_____
_____
_____
_____
_____
_____
_____
_____
_____
_____
_____
_____

On a separate sheet of paper, write down your childhood memories of what you learned about handling money and how your parents handled money. Do you see any cause or root that explains your fear or anxiety—maybe even some of your spending habits? Could it have been a learned behavior your parents passed on to you? Don't worry if you can't find a specific cause for each fear. Chances are, as you continue the program, you'll uncover many answers and solutions that will enhance your financial security.

MARY'S STORY

Mary called in to our radio show to voice her questions and concerns. She had already filed for bankruptcy twice, and she wanted to know what she could do to get back on track without repeating her past mistakes. She was afraid her past spending habits would cause her to end up with another bankruptcy.

The first question we asked Mary was "When you were young and living at home, did you typically have to beg your parents for money to get something you really wanted?" She said yes.

Next we asked, "When you left home and received your first credit cards, did you feel empowered?" She answered yes again. Free from having to beg for money, Mary felt empowered to buy whatever she wanted. It made her feel good and powerful—until the bills coming in were higher than her income.

Once Mary realized that her problem was the result of being in charge of her own money, she realized that she was out of control. This realization was her first step toward recovery. The next was learning to be responsible with her money and credit and to consequently abstain from reckless spending. She was then able to develop a workable budget and determine where she could cut spending. The feeling of power that overspending had created was replaced with accountability on where her money was actually going.

THE FEAR OF HAVING NO EMERGENCY FUND

Do you worry because you're not saving for emergencies or

retirement? There's nothing like a financial crisis to cause us to start kicking ourselves for our lack of planning.

Have you put off saving because you feel you don't have the extra money that would require? Maybe you're waiting for that magical raise that will give you the extra boost to finally start stashing your cash away. Or maybe you're waiting on the big deal just around the corner. Whatever the reason, it's time to change your thinking.

You can't afford to wait on something that may or may not happen to begin saving. Instead, think of it as paying yourself. It may help to think of your savings as a bill you must pay. Savings is a bill you must pay on tomorrow, next year, sudden emergencies, and old age. Even if you haven't saved a dime so far, you can start saving immediately. If you can spare only a few dollars a week, start with that. The important thing is to take action. You can have your company or bank deduct a specified amount from each paycheck and pretend that the amount that goes into savings doesn't exist. Do whatever works for you to convince yourself to save. You'll be pleasantly surprised one day by how much your savings have grown.

If you're going through financial challenges, look at your budget and see where you can cut back. Put that money into a savings account. If you can find an extra $166.67 in your monthly budget, you'll have $2,000 saved in one year.

THE STRESS OF LIVING PAYCHECK TO PAYCHECK

If you barely make it from paycheck to paycheck, know you are overextended on credit, and can't pay all your monthly bills, you have cause to be concerned. You're likely feeling stressed and anxious that one emergency will send you over the edge. It's imperative that you take control over your situation. It's going to take some focus and some time, but you can get your finances under control.

The most important thing for you to do is get a grip on what's happening today with your finances. Savings will come later if you're currently living beyond you means. By taking immediate action, you'll ease some of your anxiety, and this book will help you with that.

CREDIT CARD STRESS

The difficulty with credit cards is that you're doomed with them and doomed without them. Credit card companies can be your best friends when you make your payments on time. But they become your worse enemy if you're delinquent with your payments, and they'll close your account if you go for an extended amount of time without using your card.

In today's world a person needs credit to get a good FICO score on his or her credit report. Credit cards, when used properly, help raise that score. The flipside is that money trouble often starts with the use of credit cards.

The best use of a credit card is to make small purchases using the card and pay the balance in full when you receive the bill. If your payment pattern is good and you don't max out your card, your FICO score goes up. That's a win/win. The problem is that many people lose track of what they charge, and when they get their bill in the mail, they realize that the balance is more than they can pay that month. They resort to making a minimum payment. Say hello to credit card debt.

If you're using the card each month and not paying the entire balance in a timely manner, your debt is growing. That's potential disaster if your income is reduced and you owe more than you make in a month. When that happens, the credit card company is no longer your friend; and if you fall behind or make late payments, your FICO score drops, harassing phone calls begin, and your stress level rises.

If this is happening to you, you must stop using your credit cards immediately. If your credit card account is still open and you have unused credit, don't charge anything more on the card. Continuing to use the card will increase debt *and* stress in the long run.

When you rely upon tomorrow's income to pay for today's expenses, (credit card charges) you're living beyond your means. You're in denial of your current situation, which, more often than not, signals financial trouble ahead.

STRESS AND DENIAL

Denial is a common self-defense ploy people use when faced with money trouble. It's easy for them to think this is just a temporary situation, and they continue spending as usual. But when the money runs out and the credit cards are maxed out, reality sets in.

A spending issue that affects many people in a financial crisis is *binge shopping*. A binge shopper is someone who goes on a shopping spree often buying things such as clothing, jewelry, a big-screen television, electronics, or an excessive amount of household supplies and food. The binge shopper seeks refuge in purchasing these items, because it's a form of escape or denial, and the person puts off dealing directly and honestly with the present financial situation.

Some people are problem shoppers regardless of their financial situation. A peek inside the closet or cupboard of a binge shopper reveals unused items with the price tags still on. These are not things the person needs. Rather, these are things the binge shopper bought for the thrill of the purchase in spite of the long-term cost.

The prescribed treatment for this behavior is to walk away. Go home. Sleep on it. By morning, the urge will have gone away. It's time to control these urges *before* they put you in further crisis. Don't continue to act out this form of denial until you've lost everything and even more guilt sets in.

Overspending can happen when you're bored or depressed. It's easy to pretend, and it feels really good to convince yourself that you're a "big spender," carelessly buying items you're convinced will make you feel better or make people think you have it all together. Then the bill comes. For some people, the cycle repeats itself in an effort to relieve depression or boredom or panic with a good dose of shopping. But then comes the day when the credit card companies shut you down and the bills continue filling the mailbox.

But doesn't God stand ready to give us peace and happiness? Why should we find it necessary to go to outside sources to receive it? Peace that doesn't come from God—because we've manufactured it for ourselves—is a counterfeit and will disappear. God must be our source of fulfillment. No other person or thing can meet that need.

As you face challenges—especially financial challenges—it's important to stay focused and ask God to give you strength. Psalm 91:1-2 assures us, "He who dwells in the shelter of the Most High will rest in the shadow of the Almighty. I will say of the LORD, 'He is my refuge and my fortress, my God, in whom I trust.'"

OVERCOMING TEMPTATIONS

Think about all the advertisements that come at you, and think of the toll they take on your mind. *Buy and be happy!* Unfortunately, the afterglow of most purchases fades quickly. Once it's gone, you're likely to head right back out to shop some more. Maybe you're thinking, *Oh, well*—*if I'm not personally fulfilled, at least others will look at me and think I am!* Guess who's left holding the bill.

To make matters worse, most department stores offer discount incentives to entice you to sign up for in-house credit cards. Ten percent off your first purchase sounds good!

Remember: the stores aren't out to make friends and make better lives for their customers, although that's certainly what they would like for you to believe. They're out to *make money*, and they know the spending habits of a typical consumer.

Let's do some calculations. Let's say you purchase clothing that totals $120, and you use your new credit card from the department store. You get ten percent off, so you save $12. Now you're paying only $108. What a deal! And that's exactly what the stores want you to think. They count on your focusing on that $12 you saved rather than the $108 you spent. If they successfully entice you into that trap by convincing you to sign up for their credit card, you lose.

Credit card companies, as well as department stores, know how to play to your weaknesses. The credit card company knows that most individuals who will open an account to save ten per cent will not pay off the balance in full when the first statement arrives. Most department store credit cards have an interest rate of twenty to twenty-two percent. If you don't pay the balance off in full when the first statement comes due, the ten percent you saved is lost to the high interest rate you'll be paying by making minimum payments. Remember: creditors are in the business of *taking* money from you. If they convince you that they're saving you money, they've outsmarted you. Don't fall into that trap. Pay cash. Let them keep the credit card.

IMPULSIVE BUYING

Retail stores are designed to separate you from your money. Every inch of the store is arranged to get you to make a purchase. If you find that hard to believe, conduct your own experiment.

The next time you stand in line at the check-out counter, notice all the inexpensive items that surround you. There is such an assortment—so many things you might not have thought of! *Why not?* you reason. *This is such a good price. I'll buy two!* You impulsively hand them to the clerk. The retailer comes out on top, because you just added a couple of bucks to what you intended to spend. Think twice before you buy.

TOUGH TIMES TIPS

Facing fear is always tough. We guarantee that the fear and stress will begin to fade once you start breaking your old habits of spending and begin to implement a plan for turning your finances around. You'll break the hold of fear and begin to walk in faith that God will help you. Facing your fears is just the beginning; taking the steps with God will empower your success. Remember: God gives peace of mind.

By establishing a plan, you'll gain the edge you need to be successful in managing your finances. The sooner you take action, the better you'll feel.

FIGURE OUT HOW YOU BLEW IT

Do not be anxious about anything,
but in everything, by prayer and petition, with thanksgiving,
present your requests to God.
—Philippians 4:6

Part of dealing with a financial meltdown is stepping back and examining how you got where you are. Are you an example of your parents' habits with money? If your parents were spenders, you may very well be a spender too. If they were frugal, you may have picked up that trait. Proverbs 22:6 says, "Train a child in the way he should go, and when he is old he will not turn from it." That, by the way, pertains to most of life, not just finances. In most marriages one spouse is usually a spender and the other one isn't. Again, this is learned behavior and training.

It's not unusual for debt to begin accumulating during our teen years and last well into adulthood. Habits are hard to break. Financial responsibility is not taught in school and is often not taught at home either. To young people who have not been taught better, small payments sound like a good way to have what they want immediately. The trap gets set, and instant gratification takes control.

Credit solicitations are routinely sent to high school seniors, and college students are hammered with credit card offers.

It's interesting that different age groups tend to view credit cards and the setting of financial goals differently according to their age.

Many of our parents and grandparents who lived through the Great Depression tend to go with one of two extremes. They're either spenders or are very frugal with their money. The spenders bought in to the "Why should I save?—it can be gone in a minute" way of thinking. Frugal savers were the ones who thought, *I'll never be caught without money again.*

Our children are now a product of how we handle our finances. The following is a typical breakdown of spending attitudes for the different age brackets who have money.

The twenty-something group is supercharged and wants instant gratification. When they see something they want, they charge it or open a line of credit. No thought is given as to how long it will take to pay the purchases off or the amount of interest that will be paid. The thought of a possible job layoff, illness, divorce, or any other unseen emergency that might disrupt their income doesn't even cross their minds.

The thirty-something group is now getting a wake-up call from the bills that are accumulating and realize that it takes longer and longer to pay off their balances if they're making only minimum payments. This group seeks larger purchases, such as a home, furniture, and automobiles. The children have arrived. More and more charges are being made. It seems there's always an unforeseen emergency that eats up any extra money.

The forty-somethings are starting to think about the future and getting uncomfortable with their debt load. The balances never seem to dwindle. Most of their money goes to bills. They never started a savings and retirement plan, because it always felt as if there was plenty of time to plan for the future.

The fifty-something group is looking ahead to the golden years of retirement. A plan is initiated to get out debt, but they're behind in saving for the future. Real concern is building about how old they'll be when they retire, since no real plan was enacted.

The sixty-and-above group needs to have their finances in order so they can live comfortably during retirement. Debt should be at a minimum, but with the rise in food, medical, and everyday living expenses, they're afraid they don't have enough. Unfortunately, it's not uncommon for seniors to carry excessive credit card debt and to end up filing for bankruptcy.

These examples don't speak very highly of our culture's handling of debt and finances. Depending on the severity of the financial problems, the mistakes we make with debt management when we're young will follow us for many years. It's best to avoid the mistakes before they happen as much as possible and learn from the mistakes we do make so they aren't repeated.

CARL'S STORY

Carl always wanted to own his own business. He had been setting aside money to help him get started. A business plan was drawn up, and everything looked good, so he took the big step and quit his job to start the business. Carl's credit was in good standing, and he had very little debt. He owned his home and had a wife and three children. The cost of starting a business took a big chunk of the money he had saved over the years. He had to buy equipment and pay rent and utilities; telephones had to be installed, and miscellaneous supplies were purchased.

Carl ran low on cash and operating capital, so he took out two small business loans. As the business began to grow, he paid back both loans.

After two years of operating the business, Carl had enjoyed good profits, so he took out another business loan to make improvements. The problem with this was that Carl was not setting money aside for savings or a reserve. He was spending the money on luxuries for himself and his family. If he didn't have cash, he used his credit cards with the idea that he would pay the credit card balances in full the following month. The money Carl was making gave him a false sense of security.

The economy began to show signs of a downturn at the beginning of Carl's third year in business. His cash flow was cut in half. That didn't stop the bills from coming in, of course. In no time, Carl was using his credit cards to survive. He tried to keep his business running as well as cover his personal and household expenses. He didn't tell his wife the extent of the financial problems, because he didn't want her to worry, and he was in charge of paying the bills.

Pretty soon Carl was taking credit card advances to pay his business and personal expenses. His finances were out of control. As long as there was credit available on his credit cards, he continued to rob Peter to pay Paul, taking advances from one credit card to pay another card. When the day of reckoning arrived, his credit cards were charged to the limit, the bills had fallen farther and farther behind, and he was late with his mortgage payment. The "big deal" didn't come to the rescue, and with no cash reserves, he was sinking fast.

Creditors and collection agencies were calling every day, and his mailbox was full of collection notices. He tried to explain the situation to the creditors when they called, and he promised them payments. But he couldn't keep his promises.

It got so bad that whenever the telephone rang, his heart started pounding. When caller identification showed that it was a creditor calling, he often didn't answer. Fear and anxiety reached new levels. He was $65,000 in debt.

Dealing with any debt—credit cards, mortgages, car payments—can be more than just a financial burden. It can affect your home life, your relationships, your mental and spiritual well-being, and your ability to do your job, among other things. Financial overload will affect you. It's hard to make decisions when a dark cloud follows you everywhere you go. That's why it's important to stay focused and stay in prayer to clear the cobwebs from your mind.

Constantly calculating how you'll pay the bills and deal with the creditors is draining. Too much debt, even if you're paying on time, causes stress.

One of several causes of financial demise is living beyond one's means. It's important to calculate your debt-to-income ratio. If the debt is too high compared to your income, a shock is coming that will trigger anxiety and depression. When there are more bills to pay than there is money to pay them, you can be affected physically. Symptoms often include panic, heart palpitations, sleeplessness, depression, and stress.

Your home life is affected if you and your spouse don't communicate openly regarding your finances. If the spouse who pays the bills knows of the dire situation and does not tell the other spouse, sooner or later your life will blow up.

CARL'S SOLUTION

When Carl called our office, he was stressed and upset. He

didn't know how much longer he could continue living under the burden of his indebtedness. Carl's only asset was his home. He was considering selling his house—and moving into a cheaper one—to get the money to pay off his debts. Carl had lived in his home for twelve years and had a young family, so that certainly wasn't what he wanted to do.

We instructed Carl not to make an impulsive decision. We asked him to list all his regular payments, including credit card payments and house payments. They totaled $5,600 per month. We evaluated what his home was worth. The value had dropped, but he still had some equity left. He would be able to pay off his credit card debt and bank loan and set aside $10,000 for an emergency fund by refinancing his home. His total savings would be $1,200 per month.

Carl and his family were able to stay in their home and not incur the expense of moving. We also suggested to him that he add extra money to his house payment each month so the principal balance would be reduced more quickly, enabling him to pay off his home in less than thirty years.

With the pressure off, Carl was able to get his business back on track. His stress was reduced substantially, and he learned a valuable lesson on money management and his part in getting off track in handling his finances in the first place. Carl also learned not to depend on credit for survival.

ADDICTED TO PLASTIC

Paying with plastic just *feels* good to many people. Why worry about tomorrow when you can charge it today? As discussed earlier, one of the biggest problems with using credit cards is that you leave yourself wide open to impulse buying. Probably more than half of what most individuals purchase with credit cards is bought without thinking it through. For some reason, people charge purchases to their credit cards that they would think twice about buying if they had to hand over the cash.

FIGURE OUT HOW YOU BLEW IT

Picture this: You're at the mall and find something you simply must have. It's a little expensive for your budget. Hold your hands out in front of you and visualize cash in your right hand and a credit card in your left hand. Which would you use to make this purchase? More than likely, if you're totally honest, it's the credit card. That's because that would make you feel as if you were *saving* your cash. But for most of us, that's the wrong choice. If you can't afford to spend your cash, don't use your credit card. If you use your credit card, keep track of all of your charges for the month. Use an index card or the sample form in this chapter. When you reach the limit of what you can pay off in full when the statement comes, quit charging.

For example:

Date	Card Used	Item	Cost	Subtotal
Mar. 7	Visa	dinner	32.50	32.50
Mar. 10	Visa	clothes	29.98	63.48
Mar. 15	MasterCard	gas	20.00	83.48

In this example, each credit card purchase is subtotaled so you'll know how much you're spending on all the cards together. This helps you set money aside in your checking account to pay each balance off in full each month.

If a person can't seem to control the use of his or her credit card or has a problem with impulse buying, it may be because that person finds power in purchasing on credit. Perhaps he or she feels powerless in other areas of life. Using plastic makes the person feel in control or increases a feeling of self-worth. Obviously, this is a false sense of control and really a trap.

Our successes in life are really determined by the choices we make. Just about everyone possesses the intelligence to recognize a bad situation. It then becomes a matter of choice: walk head-on into a bad choice, or turn around and head the other way.

Isaiah 26:3-4 says, "You will keep in perfect peace him whose mind is steadfast, because he trusts in you. Trust in the LORD forever, for the LORD, the LORD, is the Rock eternal."

By keeping your mind focused on the Lord and overcoming temptation, you can walk away from the bad spending habits that may be gripping you

TOUGH-TIME TIPS

- Pay cash whenever possible.
- Keep an index card or registry in your purse or wallet, and write down every credit card purchase you make during the month. Charge no more than what you can pay in full at the end of the month.
- Have a cash reserve.
- Communicate with your spouse about all financial matters.
- Never use credit cards for survival bills.
- Don't rob Peter to pay Paul. In other words, don't take cash advances from one credit card to pay other credit cards.
- Communicate with your creditors.
- Don't continue to charge with the idea that things will get better.
- Don't spend extra money on luxury items unless you have a substantial cash reserve.
- If you know you're an impulsive buyer and find something you think you must have, go home and sleep on it. The urge will probably be gone the next day.

4
SYMPTOMS OF TOO MUCH DEBT

*People who want to get rich fall into temptation
and a trap and into foolish and harmful desires
that plunge men into ruin and destruction.*
—1 Timothy 6:9

Everyone desires nice things. With all the television, radio, and print advertising for luxury items such as dream vacations, luxury cars, and designer clothes, it's no wonder we get caught in the spending mind-set. American Express, MasterCard, and Visa all advertise how easy it is just to *charge* it and pay later.

The problem with these enticing ads is that they can make you believe your *wants* are actually *needs*. And needs don't feel like temptations. They feel like—well, needs. When you give in to the temptation of buying those kinds of needs by charging now and paying later, the money being spent causes a shortage of funds for other items in the budget. When you come up short, the first thing you do is cut back on your spending.

It's not unusual when this happens that one of the first things to cut back on is tithes and offerings to the church. God is put on the back burner in order to satisfy what have now become needs.

The Bible has a lot to say about money and discipline. "He who ignores discipline comes to poverty and shame, but whoever heeds correction is honored" (Proverbs 13:18). A disciplined person will turn and walk away from the temptation of buying or charging something that's not really a need.

History has shown that one can't rely on having only good economic times. Many have lost life savings, retirement funds, and homes when the economy took a turn for the worst, and those people have kicked themselves for unnecessary purchases—not to mention the credit card debt they ran up. When you're forced to face a financial crisis, it's easy to beat yourself up for any bad financial decisions you made, but that isn't really helpful. Instead, learn from your past, and start looking toward your future.

Symptoms of debt sneak up on you like the symptoms of a bad cold—first you notice a few sniffles, then a couple of sneezes, and pretty soon you're feeling achy, and you know you're sick. Accumulating too much debt is sneaky too. It is a slow-moving accumulation of the "I want" and "I gotta have it now" syndrome.

"DEBTITIS"

"Debtitis" creeps up slowly, but many people fail to recognize the symptoms until they are *debt-sick!*

All of us have dreams of buying a home, buying a vehicle, possibly starting a business, paying the bills with no sweat, living comfortably, and planning for retirement. But the dreams of a peaceful and tranquil future can be stolen away if we fail to recognize the warning signs of debt.

DISEASE OF DENIAL

When times were good, it felt as if there were no pressure to keep track of spending or to balance the checkbook. Maybe you kept a loosely structured budget in your mind somewhere, but you never felt the need to *really* adhere to it. Why should you? So you just stuck your head in the sand and figured the finances would all work out in the long run.

Continuing to deny the reality of your financial situation may cost you when you want to make a major purchase such as a vehicle or a home. When reality hits and you realize you can't make a payment for something you *really* need, it's likely that you've been refusing to face the facts for quite a while.

"BIG DEALITIS"

We've talked a little about "big dealitis"—another money disease many people suffer from. It's not uncommon when we're counseling people in financial stress that they tell us they're working on a big deal, that when it happens they'll be able to pay off all their debts and achieve financial security. Remember the folks who couldn't wait to take part in the frenzy of buying up houses and flipping them to make a fortune? Then the bottom fell out of the housing market. Or there were people who left secure jobs to join an up-and-coming company that quickly went under. Many folks put all their money into a fail-proof stock that failed. No matter how enticing it sounds, never depend on what may happen. Depend only on what you have today and, of course, God.

Any big deal should be looked at as something extra. Never quit working and run after the "big deal." If you lose sight of the here-and-now concept, you'll be chasing a fantasy that may or may not happen. Proverbs 28:19 says, "He who works his land will have abundant food, but the one who chases fantasies will have his fill of poverty." There will always be a carrot dangling in front of you, but God's Word tells us to not chase a fantasy. If it happens, great! If it doesn't, you're not out anything. Any investment of money, time, or expertise should be prayed about to see if God gives you inner peace in moving forward, remembering that He will not violate His Word. Inner peace to move forward does not mean you drop everything else, because His Word encourages us to be careful and wise and not fall for get-rich-quick schemes. You've heard the old adage that if something looks too good to be true, it probably is. That has been our experience. Also, God will give you inner peace about anything He is in. If there's uncertainty, don't do it.

I've heard of people who quit their jobs to sit and wait for God to tell them what to do. Praying and waiting on the Lord is good, but His instruction to us is to keep working and paying the bills as we wait. God will direct your path. There are no money trees in your yard. Wouldn't it be great if there were?

CREDIT CARD BLINDNESS

It's easy to put on blinders or at least very dark-tinted glasses when spending money and charging purchases. Have you ever calculated how much you're spending when you use those credit cards and make minimum payments? How about that auto loan or home equity line of credit? Most people don't give it enough thought. If you were to calculate the total cost by the time that item is paid in full, you might reconsider.

When you make a purchase on a credit card or get a loan for a bigger purchase, the lender will charge an annual percentage rate

(APR) for the use of the money. To calculate the total cost of a loan, multiply your monthly payments by the total number of months you'll be making payments. Subtract the total price of the item from the total of the monthly payments. That remainder is the total amount you will have paid in interest. Let's say you purchase an automobile for $12,000 and finance it by borrowing $10,500 at an interest rate of 7 percent, and your payment is $251.44 a month for four years (48 months). At the end of the loan you will have paid $12,069.12. You will have paid $1,569.12 in interest. Based on this example you really paid $13,569.12 for the automobile—interest plus the sales price.

Most people have no idea what the interest rate is on their credit cards. Some banks calculate interest on their cards on a daily basis, while other banks calculate interest on a prorated basis, known as a grace period. Prorated interest means that no interest is charged until the billing cycle. If the balance is paid off before the billing cycle, you had free use of the bank's money. If you don't pay off the balance on the credit card purchase by the end of the billing cycle, the interest—or finance charge—is added to the balance. Cash advances may carry a higher interest rate than purchases. Always know what you've agreed to.

Look at this in dollars and cents. If you charge $1,000 in one month for clothes and eating out and make only the minimum payment each month, it would take you approximately eleven and a half years to pay off that credit card, and you will have paid $1,104.63 in interest. That means that those clothes and meals cost you $2,104.63. *That's if you don't charge another penny* on that card during that whole eleven and a half years! Remember, too, that as your balance decreases, so does the minimum payment required.

KELLY'S STORY

Kelly came to our office for help. She was a well-educated woman who owned her own business and seemed to be in control of every area of her life with one exception: finances. As she began to share with us about her business and her frustrations with her finances, you could see that her self-confidence in the area of finances was weak.

It was apparent that Kelly felt defeated every month as she tried to pay her bills. Maybe you're familiar with that sinking feeling and the constant stress and fear she was experiencing. She was afraid somebody would find out her secret and realize she wasn't all she appeared to be—a woman who owned her own business, drove a nice car, wore nice clothes, and lived in a beautiful home! But poor money management and an overwhelming amount of debt were slowly destroying her self-image and affecting her business. Kelly was waiting for her business to take off and make her rich. She was always looking for that big deal just around the corner. She had a false sense of security and wore blinders, never seeing what was ahead. The creativity and passion for her work had been replaced by worry.

Kelly had graduated from college with $45,000 in student loan debt and $25,000 in credit card debt. She had added the cost of running her business, her house payment, and car payments. She was in a very bad place.

Every one of her credit cards was charged to the limit. Her payments were always late, resulting in late-payment fees that pushed her balance over the credit limit, adding another fee. She couldn't seem to get the extra money to pay down the credit cards. Kelly was caught in a vicious cycle. Even though she wasn't charging anything new to the cards, the balances were increasing from the finance charges, late fees, and over-the-limit fees. She was drowning.

Kelly had taken student loans and gotten the credit cards without knowing what the total cost of that debt was really going to be.

You've heard similar stories. Maybe you're living this story yourself. If you had really understood and read more thoroughly the details on the applications and contracts before signing them, you would have done things differently.

After reviewing Kelly's situation, we showed her how much she was paying for the money she had borrowed. She was astonished! Bankruptcy was not an option, because a large portion of her debt was student loans that could not be discharged.

We recommended to Kelly that she contact all her creditors to see if they would work with her in reducing her interest, thus reducing her payments. Many creditors were cooperative and agreed to do that. We also suggested that Kelly consolidate all her student loans into one loan. This reduced her payments and lumped everything into one lower payment.

By facing her fears and putting a plan into action, Kelly was on the road to recovery. Her finances became more manageable, and she was able to pay her debt off more quickly. She regained control of her life, and once her debt was reduced, she started doing the things she loved to do.

AVOID BEING OVERLY OPTIMISTIC

When you apply for credit, before the creditors approve your application, they look for two major factors:

1. Your ability to repay the debt. This is determined by your job, your employment and the length of time in your position, and, if applicable, how many years you've owned your own business. They also look at your debt-to-income ratio. It's not unusual for individuals to think they can afford a higher monthly payment than they qualify for. This again is because the hopeful borrower has not done an accurate budget and reality check.

2. Your credit history. The creditor looks at your credit and repayment history, the amount of credit you have, and what creditors you have accounts with.

Credit grantors usually estimate net income at eighty percent of gross income. Expenses should not exceed seventy percent of your net income. Variable expenses such as food, fuel, utilities, and such are estimated to be about twenty to twenty-five percent of net income. Credit-grantors prefer that only ninety to ninety-five percent of net income be committed to all expenses. If your debt is more than that, you're probably overextended.

DEBT CALCULATIONS

Most people can afford to pay ten percent of their net income to installment debt, not including mortgage payments. If you pay out more than fifteen percent, you need to cut back; if you pay out twenty percent, you're in trouble and need to stop using credit immediately; twenty-five percent puts you in deep trouble, and you'll probably need professional help and will need to drastically change your lifestyle.

Calculate these ratios at least once a month to make sure you're not getting over-extended.

SPENDING CALCULATIONS

The average American family spends about $50,000 per year. The following chart shows where the money goes.

Housing: $1,333.33 monthly, $16,000 yearly	32%
Transportation: $791.67 monthly, $9,500 yearly	19%
Food: $625 monthly, $7,500 yearly	15%
Personal taxes: $375 monthly, $4,500 yearly	9%
Family business: $375 monthly, $4,500 yearly	9%
Entertainment: $250 monthly, $3,000 yearly	6%
Health care: $208.33 monthly, $2,500 yearly	5%
Clothing: $208.33 monthly, $2,500 yearly	5%

NOTES

- Housing includes rent/mortgage, utilities, water, fuel, telephone, taxes, maintenance, repair, housekeeping supplies, furnishings, and equipment.
- Transportation includes vehicle purchases or lease, gasoline, oil, repairs, finance charges, insurance, taxes, licenses, and public transportation.
- Food includes meals, beverages, and snacks consumed outside the home—plus cereals, bakery products, meats, poul-

try, fish, eggs, dairy products, fruits, vegetables, alcoholic and nonalcoholic beverages consumed in the home.
- Personal taxes include federal and state income taxes.
- Family business includes life insurance, pension, and Social Security.
- Entertainment includes concert, movie, and amusement admission tickets; lottery tickets; club admissions; books; magazines; newspapers; toys; sporting supplies; sporting and photographic equipment; audio, video, and computer equipment and software; musical instruments; flowers, seeds, and potted plants.
- Health care includes insurance, medical services, drugs and medical supplies, personal care products and services.
- Apparel includes clothing, shoes, and accessories, laundry and dry cleaning services.

Source: United States Bureau of Labor Statistics, Consumer Expenditures

To avoid becoming overextended, use the Monthly Debt Worksheet at the end of this chapter to keep a record of your debts. Complete it each month to make sure your debt is under control—decreasing rather than increasing.

AVOIDING THE DEBT TRAP

The rich rule over the poor, and the borrower is servant to the lender (Proverbs 22:7).

It's important to have the tools and knowledge to make the right decisions when accepting credit. Don't accumulate or accept more credit than you need. If you have credit cards, keep the balances low or at a zero balance. This can increase your FICO scores, which we'll discuss in more detail in another chapter. Put the credit cards you're not using in a safe place, and use them only in an emergency. The risk associated with unused credit cards is the temptation to use them to run up more debt, increasing your debt ratio. Your debt ratio is the total amount of your debts (not including your mortgage or rent) divided by your net income (after taxes). For example, if your monthly debt payments total $600 and your income is $3,000 per month, your debt ratio is twenty percent. Remember: you want to keep your debt ratio at ten to fifteen percent of your income.

When you use your credit card, never charge an item or meal under $25 unless you intend to keep track of it and pay it off at the end of the month. It's the small purchases that add up to large balances that will take you many years to pay back. Why pay interest on a small debt for several years if you could pay cash at the time of your purchase?

Keep $1,000 to $2,000 in cash in a reserve account for emergencies. This will help you not use your credit cards. Don't carry more than three credit cards. If you do, they tempt your spending.

Never make a decision for a major purchase on credit until you've analyzed how much it's going to cost you. Go home and sleep on it. Don't make a decision at the store or merchant's place of business. Resist impulse buying.

You don't want to be in bondage to the lender by making the wrong decision.

TOUGH-TIME TIPS

- Reality checks are essential to avoid excessive debt.
- Treat the "big deal" as something extra that might come in. Don't count on it for the here and now.
- Make sure you calculate how much you're actually paying for anything you buy on credit.
- Most people can afford to pay ten percent of their net income to installment debt, not including mortgage or rent payments.
- If you pay more than twenty percent of your net income to installment debt, not including mortgage or rent payments, you're in trouble and need help.
- It's essential to keep track of your monthly payments.
- Never make an impulsive decision for a major purchase.

SYMPTONS OF TOO MUCH DEBT

Monthly Debt Worksheet

List all your monthly debts, including all credit cards, school loans, automobile loans, installment loans, and personal loans. Do not include mortgage payment or rent.

Monthly Debt Worksheet

Creditor Name	Balance	Monthly Payment
Credit Cards		
_____	_____	_____
_____	_____	_____
_____	_____	_____
_____	_____	_____
Loans		
_____	_____	_____
_____	_____	_____
_____	_____	_____
Personal		
_____	_____	_____
_____	_____	_____
Other		
_____	_____	_____
_____	_____	_____
Monthly total	_____	_____

Debt-to-Income Ratio

To determine your debt-to-income ratio, divide your monthly net income (after taxes) into your total monthly debt. The answer will show your percentage.

Net monthly income (after taxes) $_____
Total monthly debt

MONEY TROUBLE

$_____ (See Monthly Debt Worksheet for this amount.)

Formula

Use your calculator

Total monthly debt _____ divided by net monthly income _____ equals your debt ratio _____.

Remember:
- 10%   Excellent
- 15%   Fair
- 20%   Disaster waiting to happen
- 25%   Stop! Get help!

Worksheet to Assess Your Own Behavior

Answer each of the following questions—true or false

1. I don't have assets that I can use in case of an emergency.
2. I don't pay my balances off in full each month.
3. I open charge accounts to get the discount.
4. I have no idea what my debt-to-income ratio is.
5. When I shop, I find it hard to walk away from a purchase.
6. My spouse and I don't communicate about our financial situation.
7. I take cash advances from one credit card to pay on another credit card.
8. I have problems paying my bills. I am afraid to contact my creditors.
9. I don't have a cash reserve for my personal and/or business accounts.
10. When I have trouble paying my bills, I keep hoping for the "big deal" to come in.

If you answered "true" to three or more questions, you're headed in the wrong direction.

5
TALK ABOUT IT

Cast your cares on the Lord and he will sustain you;
he will never let the righteous fall.
—Psalm 55:22

Dealing with a financial crisis is paralyzing for many people. Some refuse to talk about it because they are either embarrassed or feel they can handle the problem on their own. Many people hibernate and withdraw from their friends and family to suffer in silence. None of these is a good option.

Two heads are better than one. The worry caused by financial problems puts a stress on marriages and other relationships and affects the ability to concentrate at work.

Does God care about our finances? Yes, He does. Talking to Him through prayer does wonders. Prayer brings inner peace and strength. Our motto has been "Faith, hope, and a plan." We have faith that God will see us through, hope that He will show us the way, and a plan to follow the instructions and insights He gives us.

Unfortunately, many people blame God for the mess they're in. The truth is that we usually cause our own messes. But God is there to pick up the pieces, and many people find their faith renewed during troubled times.

Often people think talking about money is taboo. It's interesting that these same people can talk to friends about current events, their families, sex, and their relationships. But when it comes to money—they clam up.

Although both men and women seem to have a hard time sharing their financial problems with others, women tend to be a little more open with other women friends about money trouble. Men play very close to the vest, feeling they'll regain control and handle their problems on their own.

At one time or another, each of us must learn about finances. Some of us have to learn the hard way. It's far easier to get the information you need and to address your fears by talking to someone about your situation. When you open up to friends or experts, you'll often discover that many of them have experienced similar challenges. Thus, they identify with your feelings and circumstances. Frequently they can give you solid advice on how to deal with the problems or where you can go for help.

Often our trials and challenges become testimonies that can help others.

Seeking outside help is nothing to be ashamed of; it's an opportunity to change your financial situation. That's why we encourage people to talk about their money issues with individuals they trust.

If you're embarrassed or feel uncomfortable talking with others about your fears and concerns regarding money, we encourage you to find someone you trust and open up to that person. Speaking with someone else and networking with other people about financial matters can be a source of both emotional support and sound advice. Discussing your finances doesn't mean revealing your yearly income or the dollar amount in your checking account. It doesn't mean telling the amount of your credit card debt. It means asking questions, outlining scenarios, setting goals, reading up on topics that interest you, surfing the Net, talking with friends, and availing yourself of professional financial advice. Doing this helps you deal with the money you do have as well as plan for you future.

Managing money takes time and effort. Whether you're trying to get out of debt or preparing for retirement, it's important to be consistently proactive with your planning. Since personal finance is a never-ending journey, expect to revisit your goals and plans to make sure you stay on track. As your situation changes, you can make revisions to your plan to fit current needs. Speaking up, networking, and finding the answers to your problems can be critical to helping you attain your financial goals.

SINGLES

If you're single and don't have a spouse to journey with you through money trouble, it's important that you reach out to a friend, family member, or financial expert to help you establish a plan that's suited to your situation. You don't have to be alone and suffer in silence.

Once you decide to enlist the help of a friend or an expert, be honest with that person. Make a list of financial goals you hope to reach; then put together a workable budget. Make a complete list of your bills and a list of your sources of income. Compile a separate list of items you purchase or charge that could be eliminated. If you're coming up short, discuss other ways to generate more money each month.

Meet with your friend or expert at least once a month for accountability and to chart your progress. Holding yourself accountable to another person will help you stay focused on your goals and be more aware of the importance of every financial decision you make.

As a single person, you should never open a credit card or line of credit for a friend or someone you're dating, not even if you feel sorry for the person because he or she is having financial struggles. There's a good chance you'll get burned and end up responsible for paying off the other person's debt and could end up seriously damaging your own credit rating.

We always advise against cosigning or opening a credit card account for someone else. Your signature implies financial accountability, and that's exactly what you'll get from disgruntled creditors if the other person becomes delinquent on the accounts—and you'll probably be the last one to find out about the delinquencies. Even if you think you're going to marry that person, don't get into a financial entanglement. Be responsible to yourself, and protect your own credit.

MANDY'S STORY

Mandy was a divorced mom with three children. Her husband had always been responsible for paying the bills, and she had no experience in handling finances. She ran up credit card debt and came up short every month in paying her bills. She didn't sleep at night because of her financial worries, and her anxiety was spilling over to her relationship with her children.

When Mandy came to our office for help, she was distraught.

She had a good job, but after reviewing her situation, we saw that way too much money was going toward incidentals for her children as well as picking up fast food when they wanted it, buying expensive clothes for them, and making other frivolous purchases.

It's not unusual for a single parent to overindulge the children to assuage the guilt he or she feels because of the divorce.

Once we pinpointed the problem, we instructed Mandy to make a workable budget. Once that was completed, she was still short $200 each month. The company she worked for offered overtime, so we suggested she put in extra hours until she could pay off her debt and live within her means.

We also instructed her to contact a close friend to confide in her about her financial situation who would hold her accountable to pay off those bills.

We heard from Mandy after about six months. She was meeting her friend regularly and would retire her debt within the year. Her friend was just the cheerleader Mandy needed to keep her on track and assure the success of her plan.

MARRIED COUPLES

When you're married, it's important that you behave responsibly as a couple regarding your finances. Open communication is a must. Financial secrets have a way of being discovered. No one likes to anticipate a financial emergency or disaster, but they happen.

Research shows that conflict concerning finances is a leading cause of divorce. Some couples fight about money nonstop. Others disagree about their differing perspectives of money management. Sometimes one spouse is a saver while the other is a spender. Without a genuine examination of their differences, most couples end up bickering and never achieving a satisfying solution. They just stifle the disagreement until the next money incident flares up, and the cycle starts all over again. There *is* another way.

MONEY CHATS

Rather than arguing and avoiding money management discussions altogether, strive to improve communication with your spouse. Set aside time to discuss your finances. A romantic candlelit dinner probably isn't the best setting, but deciding on a time when you'll be free of interruptions or distractions and can discuss money openly can be very valuable. It takes time and effort, and the conversation may be uncomfortable, but you'll find it's well worth it. Secrets create frustration and anger. Scheduling a time to talk is good, because you can get things out in the open and can work to resolve your problems. Share your concerns about issues that don't seem to go away. Create a workable budget together, and track your progress. Set agreed-upon goals. Learn to think as a couple regarding money, and pray together about your finances—especially if you're facing a crisis.

You should both be aware of how much money is in your checking and savings accounts. If both of you know how much money is on hand, it heads off the "Where did our money go?" confrontations. When one spouse is "in control," it's not uncommon for the spouse who's turning over his or her paycheck to feel frustrated when money runs low. If you review what's coming in and where it's going regularly, you'll avoid frustrations.

GETTING ORGANIZED TOGETHER

Once you've set up a time to talk about and tackle your finances together, gather up the bills, and make a list of the sources of income. Make a list of your assets and debts, and organize your paperwork. Create a system, and make sure both of you understand it and how it will function. Each spouse must know where important papers are in case of an emergency, and both of you should also have a good understanding of your financial picture.

Share your financial goals, prioritize them, and then establish how you both want to achieve them. Pool your assets. Share a joint household account, and mutually track the progress of your budget. Designate a set amount to savings, and have it immediately deducted from your paychecks. Decide what you want to save for together. When you're both openly working on a common goal, whether it's getting through a financial crisis, saving for the future, or any other financial goals, it's easier to act in unison. Teamwork is a powerful tool.

TIM AND PEGGY'S STORY

Tim and Peggy had recently filed for bankruptcy when Peggy called us wondering if there was any way they could qualify for a loan to buy a house.

Peggy told us that her husband, Tim, had always taken care of paying the bills. When Tim started falling behind in making the payments, he never told Peggy. Peggy said, "Tim was just trying to protect me and didn't want me to worry."

Tim fell farther and farther behind, and one day he announced to Peggy that they would have to file for bankruptcy. Peggy was shocked. She had no idea these financial problems had been occurring. Tim had been trying to fix everything so she would never find out or worry.

First we wondered how this huge secret could exist between them. Then we wondered how Peggy and Tim could continue to see it as Tim trying to protect her. Exactly what had he protected her from? Their credit was ruined; her faith in him was diminished. If Tim had told her what was happening when the trouble started, maybe they could have come to a mutual decision and sought outside help.

Before they could even think about buying a home, they had to reevaluate their communication skills and set up a plan to rebuild their credit and their relationship. The trust was gone, and it would take some time to rebuild it.

If they had been communicating and Tim had told her what was going on, they might have come up with a solution that would have averted their financial disaster. If Peggy had been in on the decisions, together they might have made better decisions. Even when finances seem unsalvageable, there's always a solution. No matter how impossible the situation, resolution is possible, especially with God's help.

COUPLES AND SECRETS

One way for you and your spouse to both know what's going on with your bills is to take turns paying them. It's common for one spouse or the other to be responsible for paying the bills while the other spouse prefers to remain in the dark. This is never a good idea. Both of you need to be aware of the big picture in case something happens to the spouse who has been in control. Shared responsibility protects you both from financial disaster if your spouse should become ill or die.

If your debt is getting too high, make sure you both know it. No secrets allowed! Confession hurts, but the consequences of keeping a secret will be much worse.

PAM AND DAN'S STORY

Pam called our office wondering if she could get a consolidation loan without her husband's knowledge. In the middle of the conversation there was a pause, and then she said, "I need to call you right back."

As it turns out, Dan, Pam's husband, had come home, and she couldn't talk about the problem in front of him. Pam had run up $30,000 in credit card debt. Dan assumed that Pam had been making the monthly payments, but she hadn't. Creditors were calling, and Dan's credit rating was destroyed. They had more problems than credit card debt, however.

We made a plan for Pam and Dan to get out of debt. But in the middle of our consultations with Pam, she confided that she was unhappy in her marriage. She said she had charged Dan's credit cards to the limit to get back at him.

Shortly after telling us this, Pam told Dan her true feelings. This was a turning point in their marriage. Pam resented having to assume total responsibility for their financial situation, and Dan realized that he had never shown an interest in their finances or communicated with her about money in any way. Suddenly he understood how important it was for him to be involved.

Fortunately, they were able to work things out. But you don't have to get to this desperate point to learn the importance of working with your spouse on your finances. Make it a priority to talk about money and bills regularly and to consistently share the responsibility of managing your money together.

MARRIAGE MONEY TIPS

Arguing about spending what's in the checking account is common. To avoid those arguments, some couples have been successful in maintaining separate personal accounts and putting some money into those every month for each spouse to spend however he or she desires. He may want to spend some of his personal budget on tickets to a sporting event, and she may want to spend her money on a day at the spa. These proposed expenditures may seem a little stereotypical, but the point is that each of you may want to have a little money to spend without having to give an accounting to your spouse. Having your own personal accounts makes that possible and relieves you of disagreements. Plus, the core household budget is safe.

It's a good idea to maintain separate credit card accounts too. Should anything happen to your spouse, each of you has his or her own credit. Keep your credit cards active to increase your credit score. Use them for major purchases and emergencies. Strive to keep your debt down, and agree to pay off the balances each month or as soon as you can. Establish spending limits, and stick to them. Maintaining this one area of your financial life will significantly decrease your potential for arguing. Don't forget your monthly financial meetings as well!

SENIORS' FINANCIAL CHALLENGES

Seniors who suffer from financial problems are becoming more common. Bankruptcies and foreclosures in the senior populations are on the rise. With the cost of living increasing, many senior adults have only Social Security to live on. Medical needs, prescriptions, and home repairs are overwhelming.

When facing a financial crisis, older adults have a tendency to be ashamed and embarrassed and, as a result, won't communicate. They don't want their children to know they're facing financial difficulties.

In many cases, it's their children who are causing the financial distress, which only exacerbates the situation.

If you're a senior adult, it's important to reach out to your family for support. Be honest with them about your financial situation. If you've run up you credit card balances, tell them. We often hear from the children of seniors who know their parents are struggling and want to help. The problem is that the senior adult won't be open with his or her adult children.

If you suspect your parents are struggling, confront them. Be ready to listen, and withhold judgments and lectures about their financial situation. Be a good listener, and help them come up with a solution.

As a senior, you may want to seek the assistance of a financial planner or debt management company. Don't hesitate to get answers and reach out.

Many adult children are still going to their parents for financial help. We have heard from parents of adult children who have good jobs but still go to Mom and Dad for money. With a limited income, the parents who give in to this are hurting not only themselves but also their adult children. The more you give your adult children, the more dependent they become on you financially. They'll continue to make purchases they can't afford if they know you'll come to the rescue. By continuing to do this, you're unintentionally crippling your adult children. They'll never learn to budget their money and be financially independent. If your children are experiencing financial hardship, give them what they need to survive such as money for food, utilities, medical needs, and so on. But never give them money for a credit card payment.

Seniors are embarrassed to refuse their adult children. Remember—you raised your children and sacrificed when they were young. It's now your turn to pay yourself and not be in a financial crisis. Just say no.

HELPFUL RESOURCES

Plans fail for lack of counsel, but with many advisers they succeed (Proverbs 15:22).

A number of financial specialists are available to help you gain control of your money:

- Accountants can assist you with bookkeeping as well as help you file yearly taxes.
- Tax specialists can help you with tax problems or work out a payment plan with the IRS.
- Attorneys can give you legal advice in areas such as wills, estate planning, and bankruptcy.
- Debt management companies—such as Cambridge Credit Counseling (800-208-5084)—can assist you in getting out of debt.
- Debtors Anonymous is a nationwide support program for overspenders.
- Financial brokers or investment representatives can help you with financial analysis, and they can assist you with investment recommendations.

Use discretion when consulting with professionals. Ask for referrals from someone you trust, or check their credentials. Make sure you feel comfortable working with them.

TOUGH-TIME TIPS

- "Do not be anxious about anything, but in everything, by prayer and petition, with thanksgiving, present your requests to God" (Philippians 4:6).
- God is in control, even when things feel out of control. Prayer, petitions (requests), and praise are all things God wants us to do to develop peace in our homes and lives.
- Money doesn't fix everything. If we have God, health, and loved ones, what more do we need? Money can't buy any of these things.

6

DEALING WITH COLLECTORS
HIDING WON'T HELP

> Do not be a man who strikes hands in pledge
> or puts up security for debts; if you lack the
> means to pay, your very bed will be
> snatched from under you.
> —Proverbs 22:26-27

As much as we hope they might disappear, bills will not just disappear. If only!

If you're in the middle of a financial crisis, you may have a short fuse—especially if the creditors and collection agencies are hounding you for payment. The constant phone calls and harassing letters may have you on the brink of explosion—ready to get into a yelling match with the collector. Folks who make their living collecting delinquent payments are sometimes rude and will use scare tactics to get payments. It's important for you to know and understand your rights and the best way to handle creditors, just as the collector knows the best way to get money from someone who is in a financial crisis. That's why the Scriptures talk about *advisors*.

If you're being hounded by collectors, it's important that you stay in constant prayer to know what to do and to be able to keep your emotions under control.

Remember: these people don't know you personally. You're just a name on a computer screen.

TRACKING YOU DOWN

Packing up and moving or changing your phone number and e-mail address won't deter collectors. Caller ID will let you know who's calling, but refusing to answer will eventually increase anxiety and bring tension into your home and life.

Collection agencies are very adept at tracking you down in order to collect a debt. Here are a few ways they do that.

Information from your credit application: This is the most logical way to find you. The creditor has this information in your file. It includes your full name, address, telephone number, Social Security number, employer, bank, credit references, and nearest living relative. If you've moved, there is a good chance someone listed on this credit application will know where you are. If the debt is transferred to a collection agency, the agency is given this information.

The post office: The creditor or collection agency can check the post office for your forwarding address.

Employers: Creditors and collection agencies can call your place of employment. Though most companies will not divulge an employee's personal information, the creditor can call you at work.

Neighbors: A creditor or collection agency can use a Criss-Cross or street directory published by the telephone company. This type of directory matches phone numbers to addresses. If your telephone number is unlisted, it will not appear in the directory. These directories also give the names and phone numbers of people living in your neighborhood.

Department of Motor Vehicles: In most states, an agency can get information about you for a small fee paid to the Department of Motor Vehicles.

Voter registration: Some agencies check the voter registration records in the county where you reside. If you've moved and re-registered in the same county, your new address will appear.

Banks: If you've moved and still have your old bank account, the creditor and collection agency will try to get your new address from the bank.

Credit bureaus: Some creditor and collection agencies are associated with the credit bureaus. If this is the situation, the agency will have access to your credit history. Even if the creditor or collection agency is not associated with the credit bureau, for a small fee they can enlist the credit bureau's help in locating you. This will be a red flag when you apply for credit as long as your problems are not resolved.

Internet: There are several web sites that list individuals. Check to see if you're on such a site. Three of these are <white pages.com>, <411.com>, and <people.yahoo.com>.

DEALING WITH COLLECTION AGENCIES

Remember: there's no such thing as debtor's prison. You will not be arrested. Your children will not be taken. At least none of these things will happen just because you owe money. But collection agencies can scare the wits out of people who don't know their rights.

Every state has a statute of limitations for collection efforts. After the statute of limitations has expired, creditors can no longer attempt to collect the debt. See the chart at the end of this chapter for information regarding the state you live in.

CAROL'S STORY

Carol was a single mother who had lost her job. It took her several months to find another job, and she had to take a pay cut. She was behind on her bills, and several accounts had been turned over for collections.

A collection agency called Carol and threatened to have her wages garnished if she did not pay her debt within 24 hours. Carol simply didn't have the money to pay the collection agency, and despite her pleas, the agency would not work with her.

We informed Carol that a collection agency could not garnish her wages unless there was a judgment against her. She would have to be served papers for a lawsuit and would have an opportunity to settle the account. We recommended that she get a copy of the Fair Debt Collection Practices Act and review her rights. We also instructed her to make a workable plan to pay off the bill.

There's a difference between (1) an original creditor trying to collect a debt and (2) a collection agency. The original creditor is the business or person who has extended you credit. A collection agency is an outside company hired by the original creditor to collect the debt owed.

An original creditor will make every effort to collect the debt, but when they've grown tired and frustrated, they'll turn the account over to an outside agency to recover whatever money can be received. The collection agency's compensation will be a percentage of what's collected. Prior to turning an account over to an outside collection agency, the original creditor will send you many letters demanding payment. Frequent telephone calls will be made to try to get you to pay the amount you owe.

An individual who is facing financial difficulties and cannot pay his or her bills will become more upset and frustrated by the threatening calls and constant letters.

The original creditor may give you six months to respond before turning the account over to an outside collection agency, writing it off as a bad debt (known as a charge-off), or suing you. No matter what they do, the damage has already been done on your credit report.

Collection agencies are the consumer's biggest threat with credit. From time to time circumstances can arise in an individual's life to prevent him or her from paying bills on time. The best solution is to pay what's owed and make arrangements with the creditor for repayment.

Collection agencies have been known to be ruthless in their tactics to collect a bill. It takes special types of individuals to work for a collection agency. They're usually people who are well-trained in what they do, and they're carefully screened to make sure they have a personality that allows them to wear a person down and get that money collected. Collectors work from a script that tells them what to say to overcome any objection you may have. They can be rude, insensitive, insulting, and intimidating.

It's not uncommon for a collection agency to make representations that they'll sue you or garnish your wages, or they'll use other threatening words that will scare you into paying.

You must know your rights regarding collection agencies. Lack of knowledge makes you more vulnerable and causes you more stress than is necessary. If setting up a repayment plan is an option for you, you must know how to deal with collectors in order to get a plan set. If you have no hope of even making payments, then there are steps you can take to stop the calls and letters. If you let a collection agency bully you into making payments that will make it impossible to meet your basic and essential living expenses, it can be disastrous.

YOUR RIGHTS

A federal law has been in existence since September 1977 called the Fair Debt Collection Practices Act. This law was written to protect consumers from unethical bill collectors. To receive a copy of this law, contact the Federal Trade Commission. This law gives the Federal Trade Commission the power to enforce the provisions of this act. (Go to <www.ftc.gov>.)

SUMMARY OF THE LAW

The Fair Debt Collection Practices Act came about because of "evidence of abusive, deceptive, and unfair debt collection practices that have contributed to the number of personal bankruptcies, marital instability, to the loss of jobs, and to the invasion of individual privacy." <www.ftc.gov/bcp/edu/pubs/consumer/credit/cre27.pdf>

A collection agency that communicates with any person other than the consumer to gain information on the consumer's location must identify himself or herself and state that he or she is confirming or correcting location information concerning the consumer, and only if expressly requested, identify their employer. The collection agency cannot indicate that the consumer owes any debt. The collection agency cannot communicate with post cards or use any language or symbol on an envelope that is mailed indicating that a debt is owed. If the agency knows the consumer is represented by an attorney with regard to the bill, then communication must be with the attorney only unless the attorney fails to respond within a reasonable period of time to communicate with the collection agency.

The collection agency is allowed to communicate with the consumer at his or her home only between 8:00 A.M. and 9:00 P.M., unless the consumer tells the collector differently. If the collection agency calls the consumer's place of work, the consumer can say that their employer does not allow personal calls at work. Once the consumer tells the collector to cease calling and follows up with a written letter confirming the conversation, the collection agency may not call the consumer's place of employment. The confirmation letter should be sent by certified mail with a return receipt requested. The letter should mention the consumer's rights according to the Fair Debt Collection Practice Act.

If the consumer has hired an attorney to represent him or her, and the bill collector or agency has been given the attorney's name and address, the agency may not contact the consumer unless the attorney fails to respond within a reasonable time period.

Without the consent of the consumer, a collection agency may not communicate to any individual about any past due bill other than a consumer reporting agency, the consumer's attorney, or the consumer.

The consumer can notify a collection agency in writing that he or she refuses to pay the bill or that he or she wishes the collection agency to stop any further communication. Upon receipt of this letter, the collection agency must cease further communication except to notify the consumer of any final action that will be taken. It would be wise to mail the confirmation letter by Certified Return Receipt Requested. A sample letter follows.

(Date)

Attn:

Account No. _____

Your company has made several telephone calls and sent numerous letters regarding my account at _____. I have indicated to you that I am unable to pay this bill.

This is my formal notice to you to discontinue all further communication with me. I am aware of my rights under the Fair Debt Collection Practice Act.

Sincerely,

A collection agency may not "harass, oppress, or abuse any person in connection with the collection of a debt." The specific types of harassment that are not allowed include:
1. Use or threaten the use of violence or other criminal means to harm his or her reputation or harm the property of any person.
2. The use of obscene or profane language to abuse the consumer.
3. Making public a list of consumers who refuse to pay their bills.
4. Causing the telephone to ring with the intention of annoying, abusing, or harassing any person at the called number.
5. Telephone calls without disclosing the caller's identity.

FALSE OR MISLEADING REPRESENTATIONS

1. A collection agency cannot represent to a consumer that the caller is representing an attorney or a law office.
2. The representation or implication that the nonpayment of any debt will result in the arrest, garnishment, attachment, and so on is unlawful providing the collection agency does not intend to take legal action. The threat to take any action that cannot legally be taken or that is not intended to be taken is a violation of the consumer's rights.

PAYMENT AND FINANCE CHARGES

The collection agency cannot add on any finance charges or service fee in collecting a debt unless the extra charge is authorized and signed by the consumer in the agreement creating the debt. For example, if there's a balance of $75, the bill collector cannot add on an extra $15 as a service fee.

Consumers who have issued postdated checks by more than five days to the collection agency must receive within three days prior to deposit a letter of intent from the collection agency to deposit the check.

YOUR RIGHT TO VERIFY THE DEBT

The federal law gives you the right to verify any debt you feel is not valid. When notifying the consumer in writing about a debt, the collection agency must provide in the notice the amount of the debt, the name of the creditor to whom the bill is owed, and a statement that the debt will be assumed valid unless the consumer notifies the collector within thirty days of receipt of the notice that he or she disputes the validity of the debt or any portion of the debt.

That means that if the consumer does not dispute the written request, there's no recourse. No response indicates that the consumer acknowledges that the debt is owed. However, if the consumer notifies the collection agency within thirty days that he or she is disputing this bill, the collection agency must provide to the consumer a verification of the debt and any documentation indicating the debt is owed. During that time, prior to verification of the debt from the collection agency, no further collection procedures may be taken. Remember: any written correspondence should be mailed by Certified Return Receipt Requested.

FILING A COMPLAINT AGAINST A COLLECTION AGENCY

If you feel that a collection agency has violated the Fair Debt Collection Practices Act, you may file a complaint with the Federal Trade Commission, with the Attorney General's office in your state, or with any other office that regulates collection agencies.

As mentioned, the law is very specific about what a collection agency may or may not do. Many people are not aware of their rights, and this is particularly true of low-income and non-English-speaking consumers, who are a primary target of abuse by collections agencies. It's important that you know your rights so you can hold the collection agency accountable if it or its representatives violate the law.

BEST SOLUTION

The best solution when dealing with collection agencies is to pay the bill as quickly as possible. The consumer laws are intended to assist you in taking advantage of the opportunity to work out your financial problems and pay what you owe.

If possible, find out from the collection agency to whom the bill is owed, and try to pay directly to the creditor rather than the collection agency. If the creditor accepts the payment, let the collection agency know the bill was paid. Make sure any negative reports to the credit bureau are removed. If the creditor will not accept the payment, pay the bill as soon as possible to the collection agency.

This law applies to collection agencies. Some creditors have their own collection departments or lawyers, and the federal rules do not apply.

If you feel you're being unjustly harassed, seek the advice of an attorney.

"Let no debt remain outstanding, except the continuing debt to love one another, for he who loves his fellowman has fulfilled the law" (Romans 13:8).

OLD COLLECTION POP-UPS

Occasionally, years after the statute of limitations has expired—as much as ten or fifteen years later—a collection agency will suddenly send you a letter or call you to attempt to collect an old debt. After seven years, the item has been removed from your credit report. If you pay this bill, it will show for another seven years on your credit report and affect it adversely. These companies purchase old debts for pennies on the dollar and most of the time do not have supporting documents to verify the debt. Beware of these companies, and use your discretion regarding how you'll proceed.

TOUGH-TIME TIPS

- If a collection agency calls, indicate to them that you know your legal rights. Write down the name, address, and phone number of the collector.
- Remain calm and polite during the conversation. Try to resolve the problem and make the necessary arrangements.
- If no solution is resolved and you do not wish any further discussion or correspondence from the collector, write a letter indicating that you do not wish any further discussion or communication with the collector. Mail it by Certified Return Receipt Requested. You'll probably receive one final communication from the collection agency telling you what it expects to do and possibly giving you a court date. The balance owed may be written off as a "bad debt."
- Dispute the bill with a letter. Send it within thirty days of receiving the bill. The collection agency must verify the bill. During the verification time, they cannot try to collect the bill.
- Mail the letter by certified Return Receipt Requested. Be sure to keep all copies of correspondence.
- If you have a complaint regarding the collection agency's tactics and feel your rights have been violated, file a complaint with the Federal Trade Commission and the Attorney General in your state. See <www.ftc.gov>.

Use this form to keep records of telephone calls and letters from a collection agency.

Collection Worksheet

Collection agency name: _____

Original creditor: _____

Date of first notice: _____

Date verification sent: _____

MONEY TROUBLE

Communication updates

Date: _____

Person spoken with: _____

Conversation: _____

_____

_____

_____

Name: _____

Original Creditor: _____

Date of first notice: _____

Date verification sent: _____

Communication updates

Date: _____

Person spoken with: _____

Conversation: _____

_____

_____

_____

Statute of Limitations to Collect Debts

State	Oral Contract	Written Contract	Promissory Note	Open-ended Accounts	State Statute: Open Accounts
AL	6	6	6	3	§6-2-37
AR	5	5	5	3	§16-56-105
AK	6	6	3	3	§09.10.053
AZ	3	6	6	3	§12-543
CA	2	4	4	4	§337
CO	6	6	6	3	§13-80-101
CT	3	6	6	3	§52-581
DE	3	3	3	4	§2-725
DC	3	3	3	3	§12-301
FL	4	5	5	4	§95.11
GA	4	6	6	6**	§9-3-25
HI	6	6	6	6	HRS 657-1(4)
IA	5	10	5	5	§614.5
ID	4	5	5	4	§5-222

78

DEALING WITH COLLECTORS

IL	5	10	10	5	735 ILCS 5/13-205
IN	6	10	10	6	§34-11-2
KS	3	6	5	3	§84-3-118
KY	5	15	15	5	§413.120
LA	10	10	10	3	§3-118
ME	6	6	6	6	§5-511
MD	3	3	6	3	§5-101
MA	6	6	6	6	c.260, §2
MI	6	6	6	6	§600.5807
MN	6	6	6	6	§541.05
MS	3	3	3	3	§15-1-29
MO	5	10	10	5	§516.120
MT	3	8	8	5	27-2-202
NC	3	3	5	3	§1-52(1)
ND	6	6	6	6	28-01-16
NE	4	5	5	4	§25-206
NH	3	3	6	3	382-A:3-118
NJ	6	6	6	3	25:1-5
NM	4	6	6	4	§37-1-4
NV	4	6	3	4	NRS 11.190
NY	6	6	6	6	§2-213
OH	6	15	15	6	§2305.07
OK	3	5	5	3	§12-3-95
OR	6	6	6	6	§12.080
PA	4	4	4	4	§5525
RI	10	5	6	4	§6A-2-725
SC	3	3	3	3	SEC 15-3-530
SD	6	6	6	6	§15-2-13
TN	6	6	6	6	28-3-109
TX	4	4	4	4	§16.004
UT	4	6	6	4	70-09a
VA	3	5	6	3	8.01-246
VT	6	6	5	3	§3-118
WA	3	6	6	3	RCW 4.16.080
WI	6	6	10	6	893.43
WV	5	10	6	5	§55-2-6
WY	8	10	10	8	§1-3-102

7

PROBLEM HOME LOANS

Trust in the Lord with all your heart and lean not on your
own understanding; in all your ways acknowledge him,
and he will make your paths straight.
—Proverbs 3:5-6

After the mortgage crisis was well underway, which actually began with the sub-prime meltdown in 2006, many people found themselves wondering what went wrong. What could cause some of the nation's largest lenders to close their doors? There are many different theories about why this happened, proposed by experts in the industry. We believe part of the problem had to do with the types of loans that were offered by banks and financial institutions. As the housing market was exploding and prices were rising, many lenders offered enticing loan programs for borrowers with credit challenges, low FICO scores, low incomes, and no down payments. When real estate prices began to fall, these loans created havoc for borrowers who needed to get out of these kinds of loans. Borrowers were unable to qualify for new loans, and that increased the number of foreclosures and bankruptcies across the country.

Let's examine some of the problem home loans previously offered by lenders.

SUB-PRIME LOANS

Sub-prime loans were made to consumers who had low FICO scores, previous bankruptcies, or past credit problems. The interest rates on these loans tended to be higher than traditional mortgages and usually carried a pre-payment penalty, meaning the loan could not be paid off through a refinance or sale for a certain amount of time, usually two or three years. These sub-prime loans typically were made with fixed interest rates for only the first two or three years, and the rates were adjusted at the end of the fixed period. Many of these lenders gave loans for up to one hundred percent of the value of the property that was being purchased or refinanced.

LOANS MADE WITHOUT DOCUMENTATION

These lenders offered loan programs to borrowers who did not have to prove income, assets, or employment. The lenders made the loan based only on the borrower's credit score and credit history. These loans were used to purchase or refinance properties.

ADJUSTABLE RATE MORTGAGES

Adjustable rate mortgages, known as ARMs, became increasingly popular as a way for a borrower to qualify for a higher loan balance than the thirty-year or fifteen-year fixed mortgage offered. Many ARM programs offered a low teaser interest rate, which translated into a fairly low payment. Some of these loans were fixed for a certain period, such as three, five, seven, or ten years. After the fixed period, the interest rate became adjustable. For many borrowers, once the interest rate began to adjust, their payments skyrocketed.

OPTION ARMS

Option ARMs, also known as pick-a-payment or pay option loans, gave the borrower four options for payment each month: minimum payments, interest-only payments, fifteen-year amortized payments, and thirty-year amortized payments. The minimum payment was the lowest available and did not fully cover the interest that was accrued during the payment period. Option ARMs became a problem when borrowers got into the habit of regularly making the minimum payment, creating a negative amortization, meaning the loan balance was going up instead of down. When the minimum payment was made, the difference between the payment and the accrued interest was tacked onto the loan balance. Once the balance reached a predetermined limit, the loan was re-cast, and new payments were calculated based on the balance and the amount of time left to pay off the loan. In most cases, when the loan was re-cast, the payment shot higher. When real estate values began to decline, many homeowners with these types of loans found themselves in trouble.

MATT AND GWEN'S STORY

Matt and Gwen owned their own business. Almost two years before they purchased their home, they had to file bankruptcy due to their financial situation. They thought their dream of homeownership was several years away until they heard of loan programs for people with less-than-perfect credit. Matt and Gwen met with a loan officer who explained the details of a sub-prime loan and informed them that it was okay to be self-employed, that their income would be stated on the loan application and they would not have to provide tax returns. They were thrilled.

However, the decent interest rate on their loan would remain at that low rate for only two years. During that time, their business began to suffer as the economy took a downward turn. When it came time for their interest rate to be adjusted, the monthly payment went up almost $1,000. Matt and Gwen tried to refinance, but their past credit history and the low value of their home prohibited them from doing so. They ended up losing their home to foreclosure and rented a less-expensive house nearby. Even though they lost their home, they kept the faith that they would eventually be able to rebuild their financial picture and get back on track.

WHAT YOU CAN DO IF YOU HAVE A PROBLEM LOAN

You may feel discouraged after reviewing the loans we identified as problems. But there are options available that may help you get into a more secure situation with your loan.

Lenders have gone back to focusing on the traditional types of loans used for purchases and refinances. These include conventional, FHA, and VA loans that come in the forms of fifteen-year fixed mortgages and thirty-year fixed mortgages, with some loans spread over forty or fifty years.

Conventional loans: There are two different types of conventional loans that are non-governmental loans: conforming and non-conforming. A conforming loan has certain guidelines set by Fannie Mae (FNMA) or Freddie Mac (FHLMC). With a conforming loan, you're able to borrow up to an amount set by FNMA or FHLMC. The other type of conventional loan is known as a jumbo or non-conforming loan. A jumbo loan is any loan that has a balance higher than the limit set for conforming loans. Both conforming and jumbo loans are available with fifteen-year or thirty-year loan terms and carry fixed interest rates.

FHA loans: FHA loans are funded by a lending institution and insured by the United States Department of Housing and Urban Development (HUD). There are many benefits offered with FHA loans, including a down payment as low as 3.5 percent of the purchase price. FHA loans have less stringent credit requirements than conventional loans. The interest rates are highly competitive. Many borrowers who would previously have used a sub-prime loan have been turning to FHA loan programs as an attractive alternative. With FHA loans, a borrower can qualify just two years after a Chapter 7 bankruptcy was discharged, and only twelve months of payments are needed for a Chapter 13 bankruptcy. If a borrower has a past foreclosure, only three years need to pass before qualifying for an FHA loan. Individuals who are going through debt management or credit counseling services can qualify for FHA loans after being on the program for one year with verification from the company that payments have been made on time. Guidelines may change; contact an FHA-approved lender.

VA loans: VA (Veterans Administration) loans are specifically designed to assist veterans with obtaining a reasonable home loan. VA loans are made by lenders but guaranteed by the Department of Veteran Affairs. A veteran can use a VA loan to purchase a home with no down payment. The closing costs are limited by guidelines established by the VA, which protects the veteran from unnecessary closing costs and expenses. These loans are not driven by credit scores, but there are some requirements to qualify. Similar to FHA, a VA borrower can qualify if two years have passed since a Chapter 7 bankruptcy was discharged, with some exceptions. If a borrower has filed for Chapter 13 bankruptcy, only twelve months of payments on the plan need to be paid in order to be eligible for a VA loan. Guidelines may change; contact a VA-approved lender.

Reverse mortgages: A reverse mortgage is a good tool for senior citizens who are older than 62. There is no monthly payment due, and the proceeds can be used to pay off an existing mortgage, get cash, or use as extra income. There are several alternatives to making a monthly payment. If no payments are made, the principal balance is increased, but the borrower does not have to worry about losing the home in foreclosure. A reverse mortgage can be either an adjustable or fixed-interest rate. Most reverse mortgages are FHA or HUD loans.

JOE AND KELLY'S STORY

Joe and Kelly were purchasing their first home in a relatively expensive area. They were nervous about the new payment, which is why they opted to use an Option ARM loan to purchase the home. They loved their loan, because it gave them flexibility to make smaller payments if necessary. However, just like many other borrowers who took out this type of loan, they yielded to the temptation to make only the minimum payment. Within a couple of years, the loan was recast, and their payments increased dramatically. Their first reaction was panic. They knew they couldn't afford to stay with the Option ARM loan, but they were unaware of their options. Fortunately, their home had appreciated enough that even with the increased loan balance, they were able to refinance into a thirty-year fixed conventional loan. The payment was higher than the minimum they were accustomed to, but by budgeting and cutting back in other areas, they were able to comfortably make their new payment.

SHEILA'S STORY

Sheila, a single mother, refinanced with an adjustable-rate mortgage because of the initially low payment. Everything was going smoothly with her loan until the interest rate adjusted. Her payments increased and became a financial burden. Sheila was worried that she wouldn't be able to qualify for a new loan because she had been late on a couple of credit card payments since her last refinance. When she contacted a local mortgage company, she was told that she qualified for an FHA loan. She was happy to find that the interest rate was low with an affordable payment. She refinanced into a thirty-year fixed FHA loan.

If you're currently in a loan that is adjusting or you have a payment that's more than you can afford, find out if you can refinance your home. Contact a mortgage company in your area, and see what types of loans you qualify for. Many people are surprised to find out that the payments on a fixed-interest rate are affordable.

The mortgage company will look at your financial situation to determine your qualification. They'll review your employment, income, credit history, and property value.

One of the main factors in qualifying for a purchase or refinance has to do with your debt-to-income ratio. This ratio is calculated by totaling all your monthly debt, which includes such items as your car, credit card payments, alimony, child support, and the monthly payment of the proposed mortgage. The total is then divided by your gross monthly income—the amount you bring in before taxes. Most lenders will not lend you money if the ratio is over 50 percent.

Since credit history is also a major component in qualifying for a home loan, it would be wise to obtain a copy of your credit report before you apply to refinance you current home or purchase a new one. Get a copy of your credit report from all three of the credit reporting agencies—TransUnion, Equifax, and Experian.

By reviewing your credit report before applying for a home loan, you can identify any errors on your report that could prohibit you from qualifying. If you find inaccurate information on your report, you can and should dispute it. In the chapter titled "Building Your Credit Report," you'll find information on how to handle credit disputes.

If you find out that you're unable to refinance your problem loan, other strategies are available that will be discussed in an upcoming chapter on saving your home from foreclosure.

TOUGH-TIME TIPS

- Remember that options are available for borrowers with problem loans.
- If you have a loan that has become a financial burden, look into refinancing. Several loan programs offer affordable, fixed payments.

8
AVOIDING FORECLOSURE

The Lord gives wisdom, and from his mouth come
knowledge and understanding.
—Proverbs 2:6

The prospect of facing foreclosure on your home loan is frightening and overwhelming. Not only do you fear the well-being of your family—you also worry about the consequences to your financial future. A foreclosure is a legal proceeding initiated by the lender to recover property after a borrower has defaulted on payments. Foreclosures are public notices and remain on the borrower's credit report up to seven years.

Sometimes defaulting on a mortgage is beyond the borrower's control because of illness, adjustment of the interest rate, the loss of a job, or some other unavoidable cause. Whatever the reason, even responsible borrowers sometimes find themselves unable to make their mortgage payments.

Being forced to move from your home due to foreclosure is painful and embarrassing. Fortunately, lenders offer options to borrowers to avoid the lengthy process of a foreclosure. However, it's imperative that action be taken early to avoid foreclosure.

ALTERNATIVES TO FORECLOSURE

Loan forbearance is a temporary option until another solution can be found and allows the borrower to delay or reduce payments for a short period of time. When a lender agrees to a loan forbearance, all legal actions stop temporarily. If your living expenses suddenly increase or if you have a loss of income, contact your lender to see if you qualify for a loan forbearance. This will give you time to get your finances back in order.

Short refinance refers to the refinancing of a mortgage by another lender for a borrower who is currently in default or has a balance higher than the appraised value. In this transaction the existing lender agrees to discount the balance that is owed on the property and take a lesser amount for a payoff of the existing loan amount. The difference between the amount owed and the payoff the lender is willing to accept is usually forgiven, meaning that you're not responsible for the shortage. This option allows you to stay in your home and obtain a more affordable home loan. To pursue this alternative, contact your lending institution to see if it's willing to entertain a short refinance; then you need to get approved for a new loan. The entire process takes several weeks.

Loan modification completely changes the original agreement between you and the lender. It's a written agreement that makes permanent revisions to one or more of the original terms of the loan. A loan modification allows you to bring your account current and avoid foreclosure if you're delinquent with your payments. However, you don't have to be delinquent to get a loan modification.

There are many different forms of loan modification, including a reduction in your interest rate, a discounted loan balance, a longer repayment term, or a combination of any of these. The type of loan modification plan differs depending on the lender's policies. These plans are ideal if you have an adjustable-rate mortgage that has an increased payment, if you've experienced a drop in income, or if you've seen an increase in expenses. It typically takes between two to four months to implement a loan modification plan.

Short sale allows you to sell the property for less than you owe on the loan. With a real estate market that is declining, this alternative is an attractive one if you've lost a lot of equity. In a short sale, the property is sold to a third party, but the transaction must be approved by the lender. Basically, the lender accepts a discount on the mortgage to avoid a possible foreclosure or bankruptcy. The proceeds of the sale go to the lender. Because you're unable to keep the property, this option is ideal only if you're willing to give up your home.

RYAN AND LISA'S STORY

Lisa was laid off from her job, and it took her several months to find a new job, which paid significantly less. During that time, Ryan and Lisa fell behind on their mortgage payments. When they came to us for help in evaluating their situation, it didn't take long to realize they could not afford their home, even with Lisa's new job. We suggested they contact a local realtor for help in selling their home. The realtor informed them that their home was worth less than the amount they owed on it and recommended a short sale. The realtor found a buyer, and the lender agreed to the short sale transaction. Ryan and Lisa were able to avoid foreclosure and rent a house for an amount they could afford.

Deed in lieu of foreclosure avoids the expensive foreclosure process if the lender will accept it. When offering a deed in lieu of foreclosure, you give the property back to the lender to release your mortgage liability. All of your interest is conveyed to the lender to satisfy your loan that was in default. In addition, to avoid the expense of a foreclosure proceeding, lenders sometimes accept deeds in lieu of foreclosure to reduce the amount of time for repossession, and this eliminates the risk of your filing for bankruptcy. As a borrower, you can benefit from this option by avoiding a foreclosure that will hurt your credit and go on public record. Your financial obligation to the lender is then released.

Lease purchase is not an option offered by lenders and is actually a real estate transaction. With a lease purchase, the buyer pays the seller option money for the right to purchase the property at a later time. The purchase price and lease payment are agreed upon. The lease term is usually one to three years. The seller's loan stays in place, and the lease payment made by the buyer is used to cover the seller's mortgage payment. No one else can purchase the property during the lease term, and at the end of the lease the buyer has the right to purchase the property by obtaining new financing to pay off the seller's loan. A lease purchase is something to consider if you're unable to sell your home outright. Many buyers like lease purchases, because it gives them the chance to get into a position to qualify for a loan. As the seller, you benefit by having your mortgage payment covered and collecting option money. If you decide to sell your home on a lease purchase, it would be wise to involve a licensed real estate agent who can help you with the lease purchase contract.

COMMUNICATING WITH YOUR LENDER

There are alternatives to foreclosure, but only if you communicate with your lender. When you make the initial contact with the lending institution, ask to speak with someone in the Loss Mitigation Department. That is who you will be working with to develop a plan to avoid foreclosure. Be sure to have the following items available during your conversation:

- Loan number
- Social Security number
- Property address
- Status of property
- Financials

During the initial conversation, note the name of the loss mitigator, and ask if he or she has a direct number for you to call with future questions. Find out if the lender requires a specific package to be completed to determine what options are available to you. The lender may have a fax number where you can send back the completed package, or you may be required to mail it back.

After completing the required paperwork, follow up; but don't call every day. The department handles many cases, and it's not a good idea to become an irritant. We recommend that you call no more than once a week regarding the status of your paperwork.

You can do the entire process directly with the lender, or you can hire a professional to help you. The advantage to hiring a professional is that he or she will know what lenders look for and how to properly fill out the required paperwork.

REQUIRED DOCUMENTS

It's crucial to carefully review and complete all paperwork the lender sends you and provide all requested documentation. Be as accurate as possible on the financial statements, as the lender will pull your credit details to verify the information. Account for all of your expenses, including food, utilities, insurance payments, transportation, and other bills you pay monthly. You'll be required to submit a hardship letter detailing the reasons you've defaulted on your loan. Provide specific dates and times relating to your hardship. Don't make up a story; be as honest as possible. If the lender discovers that you were not truthful in your letter, the lender may not be willing to work with you. You should also provide documentation supporting your letter.

The lender may ask you for paycheck stubs, bank statements, tax returns, and mortgage statements. You'll find a Document Checklist Form at the end of this chapter to help you keep track of any requested documentation.

The process to determine your eligibility for an alternative to foreclosure is similar to applying for the mortgage itself. The main difference is that when you're applying for a mortgage, you're trying to show that you're capable of making the payments. When you're applying for an alternative to foreclosure, you're trying to show that you're in a financial hardship.

If your bills are more than your income, you won't qualify. The lender wants to see that you have money left over each month. It can be as little as $200. Each lender has its own criteria.

You can avoid foreclosure, but you need to be proactive and take immediate action. Remember that the lender also does not want the property to go into foreclosure so will usually be willing to work with you if possible.

TOUGH-TIME TIPS

- By understanding the various alternatives to foreclosure, you can take appropriate measures to save your home and credit report.
- Take immediate action when you're unable to make your mortgage payments, but also remember that it takes time to implement a plan.

Document Checklist Form

Lenders will request copies of the following to review:

Payroll stubs and/or proof of income for the last 30 days (If you're paid every month, you'll need at least two months of pay stubs. If you're self-employed, you'll be requested to supply a profit-and-loss statement showing a profit or Schedule C.)

Bank statements for two months will be requested, or a letter stating that you currently don't have a bank account.

Federal income tax returns and all schedules for the last two years or a letter stating that you did not file income taxes.

Mortgage coupon of rental properties.

A detailed letter of hardship. Give details of dates and the reason for delinquency, what you have done to attempt to work out these problems, and what you have done to prevent this from reoccurring in the future. This letter is very important.

Supporting hardship information that includes a letter of termination, lay-off notice, letter from a doctor, medical documentations, and so forth.

Financial Worksheep

Assets			
Description	Borrower	Co-Borrower	Total
Checking Account	$	$	$
Savings Account	$	$	$
Cash	$	$	$
Certificates of Deposits (CD's)	$	$	$
401K/IRA/Retirement Account	$	$	$
Primary Home	$	$	$

MONEY TROUBLE

Other Real Estate	$	$	$
Automobile 1	$	$	$
Automobile 2	$	$	$
Other Assets	$	$	$
Total Net Value Assets			$

Monthly Income

Description	Borrower	Co-Borrower	Total
Gross Income	$	$	$
Overtime	$	$	$
Commissions/Bonuses (Calculate to Monthly)	$	$	$
Rental Income	$	$	$
Other Income/Specify (Child Support, Alimony, Rental, Other)	$	$	$
Less: Federal Income Tax	$	$	$
State Income Tax	$	$	$
Other	$	$	$
Monthly Net Income	$	$	$

Monthly Expenses

Description of Expenses	Monthly Payment	Total Balance Due	Months Remaining
Mortgage 1	$	$	$
Mortgage 2	$	$	$
Property Tax	$	$	$
Homeowners Insurance	$	$	$
Flood/Windstorm/Earthquake Insurance	$	$	$
Automobile Loan 1	$	$	$
Automobile Loan 2	$	$	$
Automobile Insurance	$	$	$
Automobile Maintenance	$	$	$
Gasoline/Parking	$	$	$
Other Loans	$	$	$
Credit Cards: (Visa, MC, Dept. Store)	$	$	$

Utilities: (Electricity, Gas, Water, Trash, etc.)	$	$	$
Cell Phone	$	$	$
Medical/Dental/Life Insurance	$	$	$
Medical Expenses (not covered by insurance)	$	$	$
Groceries	$	$	$
Entertainment	$	$	$
Child Care	$	$	$
School Tuition	$	$	$
Alimony/Child Support	$	$	$
Clothing	$	$	$
Other	$	$	$
Total Expense	$	$	$

Please briefly explain your reason for delinquency:

_____

_____

Total Monthly Expenses: _____

Surplus/Deficiency: _____

ALTERNATIVES TO BANKRUPTCY, EVICTION, LAWSUITS, OR REPOSSESSION

> Make plans by seeking advice:
> if you wage war, obtain guidance.
> —Proverbs 20:18

Scripture has a lot to say about the importance of seeking wise advisors. By following good advice, you can avoid losing your vehicle, being evicted, being sued for credit card balances, or filing for bankruptcy.

As you're facing difficult decisions, it's important to stay focused and seek God's direction. Going in the wrong direction can affect your life for many years. It's important to make good decisions and not go for a quick fix or easy way out.

You can't make your bills go away by ignoring them. While it's true that some creditors might write off the balance, that's not something you should count on. Plus, those would appear as charge-offs on your credit report.

There are places you can go for help.

CREDIT COUNSELING COMPANIES

If you're having trouble paying your bills and don't know how to make things right, a credit counseling company may be your solution. You should consider contacting a nonprofit credit counseling company to consolidate your debt if you're delinquent in your payments, overextended with your credit cards, or tired of paying high interest rates.

Credit counselors are noted for their ability to rebuild your relationship with your creditors through communication. They will help you work out your problems and develop a repayment program that's satisfactory to both you and your creditors.

Most credit counseling companies are nonprofit. They receive a small monthly donation from the consumer and a small percentage (called the fair share) is paid to the credit counseling company from the creditor.

When you contact a credit counselor have a list of your bills ready with the creditor's names, balances owed, and payments due. Also have your income information and a list of your living expenses available. The counselor will look at your income, assets, debts, and expenses to determine what you can afford to pay. If you've received late notices, payment demand notices, collection notices, legal suits, or court judgments, have that paperwork available for the counselor to review. The counselor needs to see the whole picture in order to develop a payment plan that will help you and satisfy the creditors.

After the counselor has received all the required information regarding your financial situation, he or she will contact your creditors to work out a repayment schedule. Most creditors are eager to work with a credit counseling service, because they know that you're seeking help and not filing for bankruptcy. If you file for bankruptcy, they know they won't collect the debt.

The credit counselor will work with the creditor to lower the payment by reducing the interest, usually to somewhere between zero percent to eleven percent. The new, lower payments will apply more toward your principal, allowing you to pay off your debts in much less time. That will save you thousands of dollars in interest, plus you'll be free of debt. Late fees and over-the-limit fees will cease to accrue when you work with a credit counseling company. If you're late, the account will be re-aged and brought current.

You'll make one payment to the counseling service to cover all your debts, and the counseling company will disburse payments to your creditors. That allows you to know exactly how much you'll be paying toward debt reduction every month and that the balances will diminish. You'll see light at the end of the tunnel.

SURVIVAL REMEDIES

While some situations require credit counselors, there are also many situations you can handle on your own. Here are some suggestions to help you determine what's right for your particular situation.

Mortgage payments: Above all other bills, your mortgage payment must be paid, preferably when due. If you don't make your house payments, you risk foreclosure. That's the last thing you want to happen.

If you're in over your head, you might consider selling the

house, but this should be done before you fall behind if possible. If you have equity in the house, you can use that money to purchase or rent another home. Remember: if the payment has not been delinquent, your credit report will not be affected.

If you've missed one or two payments, the lender will usually accept nothing less than the full amount that's past due. For example, if you missed one payment, and your next payment is due, the lender will accept the payment that is due only if the missed payment is included. If the delinquent payment is not included, the lender may not accept your current payment.

Contact the mortgage company immediately if you foresee a problem in making a house payment or if you've missed payments. Stay in communication, and see if a repayment plan can be set up. If you've fallen behind, the lender may allow you to increase your monthly payment by adding your delinquent payment to the payment due. For example, if you missed one payment of $1,000, you would add an additional $100 to your payment for a total of $1,100 for ten months. At the end of the ten months, your payment would be current. A loan modification may also be possible.

Rent payments: If you're renting and you foresee that your rent is going to be late, contact the landlord and explain the problem. Remember that the landlord is probably making payments to a lender on the home you're renting and counts on your rent to make that payment. If you're going to be only a couple of weeks late in paying, the landlord may be willing to work with you. If you have a history of paying on time in the past, the landlord may allow you to make partial payments. For example, he or she may accept a payment every other week until you catch up.

It's more cost-effective to the landlord to keep you as a tenant rather than evict you. He or she wants to avoid a prolonged vacancy that could be costly. If the landlord agrees to work with you, mail a certified letter stating the approved arrangement with a return receipt request.

If you're unable to keep the arrangement, look for a cheaper home or apartment. Do it before you fall behind so you'll have a good reference from your current landlord.

Automobile payments: If the company that has financed your automobile feels threatened that you're not going to make your payments on time, repossession can be instigated. Always contact the lender immediately if you know your payment is going to be late. Most lenders will work with you. Some lenders will allow you to defer a car payment for one month, sometimes more, and add it to the remaining balance of the contract. It's also possible that a lender will allow you to make interest-only payments, adding the principal to the balance due at the end of your contract. Refinancing your vehicle is another option that may help you reduce your payment. Do this only if your payment is reduced. You'll have additional months to pay on the loan, but it can take the pressure off until you get back on your feet.

If the payments are too high, sell your car. Take the proceeds of the sale, pay off your loan, and apply the difference to a vehicle that's more affordable.

A repossession on your credit report will hurt your chances of getting another vehicle for several years. Also, if your lender repossess your car and sells the vehicle to someone else for less than you owe on the car, you will owe the difference; this is called a deficiency judgment. This would be noted on your credit report, plus the lender will still try to collect this from you.

Secured loan payments: Secured loans are for items such as jewelry, electronic equipment, or furniture—the financed item is used as collateral. If you don't make the payments, you'll lose the item that was pledged as collateral. If you have this type of loan, be sure to communicate with the lender and negotiate your payment arrangement to reduce your payments.

Unsecured credit and charge payments: Most credit card companies won't work with you to reduce your payment until you've fallen behind. When negotiating with a credit card company, call them and let them know your situation. It's better to do this before you fall behind so they can place a note or statement in their files.

If you see that you're spiraling downward with your finances and you're not sure how you're going to come out, keep the payments on one credit card current. This one credit card can help you on your road to recovery. You also need one credit card for identification to reserve a hotel or rental car. Keep a credit card that's not issued by the same company that issued the card you're behind on; the company may eventually close both accounts.

If the credit card company agrees to accept lower payments, have them put that agreement in writing. Occasionally a creditor will allow you to make a payment of two or three percent of the outstanding balance without a finance charge.

Most credit cards are unsecured, meaning that the lender can't take items from you that were charged on the account. Their only recourse to collect is to sue you and get a court judgment. Seldom do things go that far. They will either charge off the account or turn it over to a collection agency. Of course, this will result negatively on your credit report.

The older the delinquency, the more leverage you have to negotiate a settlement with the creditor. They are more receptive to a settlement offer after the account is four to six months delinquent. After six months, the creditor will charge off the account or turn it over to a collection agency. Most creditors will work with you if you get assistance from a credit counseling company for debt management.

Student loans: Contact the lender to see if you can get the student loan deferred by explaining your financial hardship. If the lender sees that you have a legitimate reason for not paying, it may postpone the payment. The interest will continue to accrue until you begin making the payments. Review your original loan agreement to determine the lender's policies regarding deferments and delinquent accounts. Stay in contact with the lender.

Taxes: Don't avoid any communication with the IRS or your

state if you owe back taxes. The sooner you set up a repayment plan, the less stress you'll have to deal with.

The IRS and state both have an Offer in Compromise program. If you feel you qualify for this, contact a specialist—your accountant, tax attorney, or enrolled agent—to help you with the paperwork.

You can try doing this yourself, but a specialist will know the best way to approach these agencies and will save you hundreds or thousands of dollars. It's worth the investment.

If you don't respond to the letters regarding the back taxes you owe, you run the risk of having your wages garnished, your bank accounts levied, a tax lien being filed, or your property being seized. Interest and penalties will continue to accrue until the taxes are paid in full. The government will take your tax refund and apply it to delinquent taxes. Don't wait to hear from the tax collectors. Call them first.

Insurance: Most states require that you carry automobile insurance. If your state requires it and you don't have it, you will receive a ticket if you're stopped or have an accident. You could lose your license or be taken to jail. If your vehicle is leased or you have a loan against it, the lender requires you to carry insurance. If you don't, the lender will put its own policy on the vehicle, which is much more costly than the insurance you can buy, and that will be added to your loan payments. Contact your insurance company to see if you can carry a higher deductible or qualify for other discounts that will reduce your insurance payments. Compare rates offered by several insurance companies to get the best rate.

Homeowner insurance: Mortgage companies require that borrowers carry homeowner's insurance. If you fail to cover your property, the lender will put its own policy on the property, and it will cost you much more in the long run. Contact your insurance company to see what type of policy you can carry that would satisfy your lender's conditions. Shop other insurance companies to see if you can get a cheaper rate.

Medical insurance: If you allow your medical insurance policy to lapse and you have a medical problem, you may not be able to get medical insurance in the future. Call your insurance agent to see if you can raise your deductible to reduce your rates. Do some comparison shopping to see if you can find a cheaper policy.

Doctor, dentist, accountant, and attorney bills: Many doctors, attorneys, and accountants accept partial payments. If you're having a problem paying these bills, negotiate a settlement for less than the amount owed. If a settlement is agreed upon, get it in writing, and pay it off as agreed.

BE WARY

Don't fall for the promises of debt settlement companies or home-saver scams.

Debt settlement company: A debt settlement company promises to negotiate with your creditors for a payoff that is less than your current balance. The hitch is that they require you to stop making payments on your credit cards.

The debt settlement company requires money to negotiate with your creditor. An example would be if you owed a balance of $3,000 and wanted to negotiate for an amount less than that. The debt settlement company would offer the company $1,500 to settle but would require you to pay $2,000. The extra $500 goes to the debt settlement company. There's also a monthly fee that goes right into the company's pocket.

If you want to settle an account, you don't need to pay someone else to destroy your credit by having you quit making your payments. You can settle your own accounts without the extra expense of paying a company to do it. You can make an offer with whatever you feel is fair to the company. There will be more about this in a future chapter.

Home-saver scams: If your home is in foreclosure or default, beware of a person or company promising to rescue you for a fee. There are companies that prey on people who are about to lose their homes by offering to bring their loans current in exchange for thousands of dollars. They produce paperwork that must be reviewed carefully because if you sign it you may be signing your property over to them.

If you're ever approached by a company that requires payment to save your home, seek legal counsel.

RICK AND JULIE'S STORY

Rick and Julie were in serious financial trouble. It started when Julie quit her job to stay at home with their kids. Unfortunately, two months later Rick was laid off from his job, and it took him four months to find work. During that time, Rick and Julie borrowed $8,000 from family members just to make ends meet. That wasn't enough to cover all their bills, and they stopped paying on their credit cards.

One of the companies filed a lawsuit against Rick and Julie to collect the debt. When the court papers arrived, Rick contacted the attorney's office to set up a repayment plan. Once it was accepted, the creditor dropped the lawsuit, and a judgment never took place.

By being proactive and contacting the attorney before the court date, Rick and Julie avoided a judgment that would have resulted in a lien until it was paid.

TOUGH-TIME TIPS

- Try to work out a payment plan before a lawsuit, eviction, or charge-off occurs.
- Contact a nonprofit credit counseling company to help lower your credit card payments and be debt-free in less time.
- Beware of unscrupulous companies that prey on your hardships.

10
COMMUNICATE SUCCESSFULLY WITH CREDITORS

Listen to advice and accept instruction,
and in the end you will be wise.
—Proverbs 19:20

If you find that you're unable to pay all your bills, you should contact each of your creditors. This is probably one of the most unpleasant things you'll have to undertake, but there's no way around it if you want to get out of debt and make your situation better. Even though you'll feel very uncomfortable making the calls, it will help you work through your problems and come out ahead. Pray for wisdom and courage, and just do it!

Remember 2 Timothy 1:7—"God has not given us a spirit of fear, but of power and of love and of a sound mind" (NKJV). As you begin negotiations with the creditors and work out a plan, your peace of mind will increase. If you don't face up to the inevitable, uncertainty will wear you down and steal your peace.

WAYNE AND MARILYN'S STORY

Wayne and Marilyn always had a steady income and paid their bills on time. Then Marilyn had to quit her job to stay at home with their child, who was ill, drastically reducing their income. They found themselves getting deeper and deeper into debt.

Letters and telephone calls from angry, demanding creditors came every day. The telephone calls became so frequent and harassing that George and Marilyn began screening the calls. When they knew a call was from a creditor, they didn't answer the phone. The letters from creditors were left unopened and thrown into a basket. Wayne and Marilyn felt they had taken enough abuse, yet they had done nothing to stop it.

With the stress of delinquent bills and a sick child, marital strife was sure to come. There were constant arguments about who to pay and what they going to do about their situation.

Believe this: doing nothing is the worst thing you can do. If you don't face your problems, you're powerless to solve them.

When Wayne and Marilyn called for an appointment, we instructed them to bring all their bills and nasty letters when they came to meet with us. As we went through the bills, we had them make a list of their creditors, payments, delinquent payments, number of months the bills were late, and the remaining balances.

Once we were able to see the severity of the situation, we could enact a plan. It wasn't going to happen overnight, but with a plan in place, they could work their bills and one day have them all paid off.

Wayne and Marilyn examined their finances to see how much extra they had to work with after they paid their essential living expenses. It totaled just $200 per month. We decided to take that $200 and use it to pay off one bill at a time. For example, for a bill that totaled $600, they offered the creditor $200 to pay it off. If the creditor was agreeable to this offer, the creditor sent a letter to Wayne and Marilyn stating that they would accept $200 as payment in full.

If a creditor wouldn't work with them, they moved on to the next one who would accept their offer. They knew their credit report was already ruined, so they had nothing to lose—except a possible lawsuit from one of the creditors.

With this plan in place, they were able to slowly work themselves through the disaster they faced. It took a plan and communication with the creditors to be a success. By taking control of the situation, they were able to resolve their problems and reduce their debt.

Repayment Plan of Action Worksheet

Example:

Creditor	Minimum Payment	Delinquent Payment	Number of Months Late	Balance
ABC Bank	40	80	2	2,250
Bank USA	75	300	4	4,750
Medical Bill	50	50	1	50
Collection Account	250	250	6	250

Repayment Plan of Action Worksheet

Creditor	Minimum Payment	Delinquent Payment	Number of Months Late	Balance

Talk to Your Creditors Before the Account Goes to Collection

Communicating with your creditors will help solve your problems more quickly. As your payments become delinquent, failing to communicate with the creditors will increase your anxiety. Remember: there is no debtor's prison. You will not go to jail for not paying your bills. Know your rights, and report threats by creditors to the Federal Trade Commission (<www.ftc.gov>).

By refusing to communicate with creditors, they may conclude that you have no intention of paying them and could expedite the collection process. This will only make matters worse for you.

By keeping the creditors informed about your situation, you have a much better chance of working out a payment schedule. The creditor would rather work out something with you than turn your account over to a collection agency or risk your filing for bankruptcy protection.

In dealing with creditors, you can call or write letters explaining your situation. Your problems may have been caused by a job loss, divorce, taxes, illness, or something else that has caused you to be unable to meet your financial obligations.

If you communicate with your credits by telephone, write down the date, the name of the person you spoke with, and what was agreed to during the conversation. Keep a log of all conversations. Use the following worksheet.

Creditor Communication Log

Example:

Date	Name of Contact	Conversation
6/2/09	John Doe	Creditor will accept a $200 payment instead of $400 payment.
Date	**Name of Contact**	**Conversation**

_____

_____

_____

_____

_____

_____

_____

_____

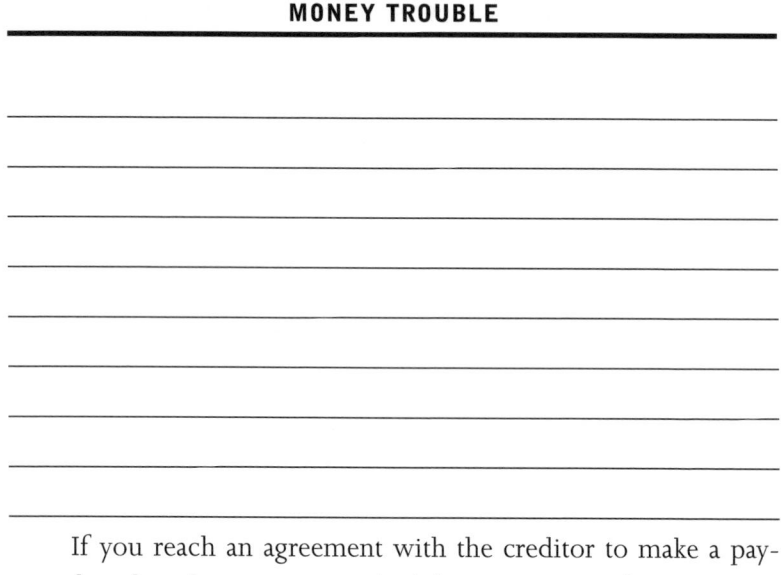

If you reach an agreement with the creditor to make a payment less than the amount required, be sure you get the agreement in writing before you begin making the payments. You don't want the creditor to report your account as a "rolling late." A rolling late means a partial payment is made that causes the account to be continuously late, and it's reported on your credit report as late.

If you communicate by letter, try to send a first payment in the amount you're proposing. This will show the creditor that you're serious about following through to repay the debt.

Pay first the creditor who's on your Priority List, Category One. The remaining creditors should be paid when you have the extra money.

Following is a sample letter to a creditor.

Sample Letter to Creditor

(Date)

Company Name

Re: Account [number]

Dear [company name],

I am your customer and have recently experienced a financial hardship. The company I work for has cut back my hours. My income has dropped, making it difficult to pay all my bills.

I am able to pay $20 per month until my hours increase. I am enclosing a check for $20 to be credited to my account. Please accept this payment and let me know if my proposal for future payments is acceptable.

Please respond in writing and make this letter a part of my file.

Sincerely,

Don Smith

MAIL LETTER BY CERTIFIED MAIL WITH A RETURN RECEIPT

NEGOTIATING YOUR DEBT

If you've found yourself drowning in delinquencies and pressure from your creditors, try negotiating with them. The more delinquent you are, the easier it is to negotiate a settlement. Negotiation is usually an option only if you're delinquent.

There's no rule about how much to offer a creditor in settlement of a debt. Creditors all have a bottom line as to how low they will go in accepting an amount lower than the full balance. Some creditors allow twenty-percent discounts, while others may discount as much as fifty- to eighty-percent.

If you don't feel that you can negotiate with a creditor, get a third party such as a friend or relative to help you, or consider hiring a credit counseling company.

Here are some guidelines to follow when negotiating with a creditor.

- Know how much you can afford to pay before making the offer. Review you finances and your budget before you call. If you don't have the money, don't make the offer. It's best to have the money in hand when you make the offer.
- The best time to make an offer is at the end of the month. If you can pay a lump sum, tell the creditor that you can pay it within three days if they accept the amount you offer as payment in full. Request a letter from them accepting your

offer before you send the money. Offering a lump sum at the end of the month is more appealing to a creditor, because it gets the account off the books.

- If you have an outstanding bill for $500 and can't pay the whole balance, offer to pay $300 over a six-month period with no additional finance charges. If the creditor accepts your offer, get it in writing before you start making the payments. Make sure the creditor's letter states that once the final payment is received at the end of the six-month period, the account will be satisfied and no additional fees will be required.
- Find out what the creditor is willing to do to ease the pressure. For example, many creditors will allow you to make interest-only payments for a limited time. Others may allow you to defer a payment for one or more months. Some may offer to settle your account by accepting a sixty-percent discount off your balance if it's paid by a certain date.
- Some bill collectors or collection agencies will mislead you. Be careful about giving them information. Never give them your bank account number or employment information.
- If the bill collector or collection agency thinks they can get a higher amount of money from you than you're willing to pay, don't back down. For example, if you know you can pay only $50 per month, and the collection agency or creditor is demanding $150 per month, stick with the $50. The agency can take it or leave it. They may say they can't accept that as payment. Mail it anyway, preferably in the form of cashier's check or money order. Keep copies of all checks. It's highly unlikely they'll return it. Be sure to mail it by certified mail with a return receipt requested. Don't let the creditor or collection agency bully you or threaten you into paying more than you can afford.
- Many creditors have re-aging programs. If your account has not been charged off or placed for collection, the creditor

may allow you to set up a new payment schedule. Once you've made the number of payments required by the creditor, the account will become current. For example, if you were five months late, the creditor may reduce your interest rate, allowing you to make three consecutive payments. If the payments are made on time, the account will be brought to a current status. Your credit report will show you as current.

If after making payment arrangements with the creditors you find you're unable to pay as agreed, immediately notify the creditor and make new arrangements. Request a letter from the creditor confirming your new agreement before sending any money, reducing the risk of the creditor denying that a new arrangement has been made.

Include in your negotiation a request that the creditor remove the negative entry on your credit report. They can do it if they choose to. Some creditors may not be willing to do this. If they won't remove it, see if they will show it as "paid" or "satisfied" rather that "settled." "Settled" is viewed as negative.

DEALING WITH COLLECTION AGENCIES

When a creditor gives up on collecting a debt from you, the account will likely be turned over to a collection agency. As mentioned before, collection agencies can be aggressive and demanding. The collection agency knows the best chance of collecting the debt is within ninety days of contact with you. From the collection agency's point of view, the longer the debt remains unpaid, the more unlikely are the chances that you'll pay. That's why the collection agency's tactics are so aggressive the first ninety days.

The collection agency will initially send you a letter asking for payment. This is followed up by a telephone call. Early conversations will be pleasant, but the longer you don't pay the bill, the more aggressive and intimidating the collection agency becomes.

When you get the first letter, review it carefully. If there are any discrepancies, you have thirty days to dispute the validity of the debt.

Send the letter by certified mail with a return receipt to the collection agency requesting documentation from the creditor regarding the bill. The collection agency must send you verification and can't continue trying to collect the debt until they've sent you such validation.

If the debt is valid, the collection agency will proceed with collections efforts. Don't make an agreement to make any payments until your essential bills are paid and you have money to work with.

If you have the cash to settle the account for less, make an offer. Don't make an offer you can't follow through with immediately. For example, if your debt is $200 and you offer $75, ask the agency for an acceptance letter, and be prepared to send the money immediately. Get the acceptance in writing before you send the money. Many people have sent payments agreed upon verbally, expecting the debt to be paid in full and settled, only to discover later that the creditor or collection agency didn't remember the agreement. Protect yourself.

If the collection agency has an account they've purchased from the original creditor, they must get an approval of any discount that's offered from the original creditor before accepting your offer.

Don't be afraid to offer less than the amount owed. In most instances, if you offer to make monthly payments, the collection agencies will not give you a discount.

The best time to make offers on any accounts with the creditors or collection agencies is at the end of the month. Most collectors have quotas they must meet. At the end of the month their goal is to have as many accounts as possible paid off.

It's important that you familiarize yourself with the Fair Debt Collection Practices Act. As mentioned earlier, you can receive a copy of this act by writing the Federal Trade Commission or by visiting the web site at <www.ftc.gov>. If you have a complaint, file it with the Federal Trade Commission.

TOUGH TIME TIPS

- Contact your creditor immediately if you're having problems.
- Get any agreement you make with the creditor in writing before making a payment or settlement.
- Don't negotiate with a creditor unless you know you can make the payments or pay the balance of the debt in full.
- Negotiate at the end of the month.
- Know your rights under the Fair Debt Collection Practices Act.

Repayment Worksheet

Make a list of creditors and collection agencies you owe. Include the minimum payment, the past due amount, the balance, and the amount you can pay. Do this every month until all accounts are satisfied.

MONEY TROUBLE

Example

Month: May

Creditor	Minimum Payment	Past Due Amount	Balance	Amount You Can Pay
ABC Bank	40	80	2,250	50

Repayment Worksheet

Month:

Creditor	Minimum Payment	Past Due Amount	Balance	Amount You Can Pay

11

PAYMENT PRIORITIES
DEALING WITH STRESS DURING A FINANCIAL CRISIS

*I will instruct you and teach you in the way you should go;
I will counsel you and watch over you.*
—Psalm 32:8

After prayerfully evaluating your financial situation, it's important to set up a workable payment plan. However, before that can be done, you must prioritize your bills, something you should do anyway, even in good times.

There are three categories to separate your bills into that will enable you to determine in what order they'll be paid.

- **Category 1: Survival Bills.** It's tempting to pay the creditors that are yelling the loudest—because you feel intimidated. That would be a wrong choice. Survival bills are ones that protect your home and family's well-being: mortgage or rent, utilities, food, and so on.
- **Category 2: Essential Bills.** Essential bills are the ones that must be paid, but not until the survival bills are paid. Examples are credit cards, unsecured loans, and medical and legal bills.
- **Category 3: Other Priorities.** These are debts that must be moved to either category 1 or 2, such as medical insurance, life insurance, child care, and clothing.

JACK AND LINDA'S STORY

Jack was employed by a company that paid him a salary and commission. His wife, Linda, worked as a receptionist part time so she could be with the children when they got home from school.

For two consecutive months Jack's sales quota was down, affecting his income. They began to fall behind on paying their bills. The creditors were calling and sending letters requesting payment.

Every time the telephone rang, Jack and Linda were overcome with feelings of dread and despair. The more aggressive the creditor's collection efforts, the more intimidated and stressed they became. The creditor causing the most stress got paid.

It wasn't long before their house payment became delinquent and rolled into the second month of delinquency. When they sent in their late house payment, the mortgage company wouldn't accept just one payment—it demanded that payment be made for both months. Jack and Linda didn't have the money to cover two payments, because they were still trying to satisfy all their creditors. Thus, the house payment rolled into the third month of delinquency. Again, when Jack and Linda sent in a payment, the lender sent it back, demanding all three payments.

The lender was threatening to foreclose on their home. Jack and Linda had to step back and reevaluate their priorities on what creditors needed to be paid first.

A priority list of their debts should have been established before they ever ran into difficulties. Developing good habits and sticking with them is essential.

Once Jack and Linda stepped away from the situation and realized that they couldn't pay everyone, they were able to catch up with their mortgage payments. Yes, the other credit card bills fell behind, but they were at least able to keep their home.

When Jack's income began to increase, they slowly brought their other accounts current, but it was a long and slow process.

※ ※ ※

"If anyone does not provide for his relatives, and especially for his immediate family, he has denied the faith and is worse than an unbeliever" (1 Timothy 5:8).

Your rent or mortgage, food, gas, electricity, water, and telephone bills are top priorities. Tithing also fits into this category.

There may be a different consequence of nonpayment for each of your creditors. It's important that you know what each consequence is.

Too often we meet with clients like Jack and Linda, who run into a money problem and pay the creditors who are calling and writing them most. This is the wrong approach.

While there are three categories of bills, the goal is to get all the bills from Category 3 placed into either Category 1 or 2 so that you're essentially working from only the first two categories.

CATEGORY 1: SURVIVAL

The first category is a debt or expense that must be paid in order to protect your home and family's well-being and be obedient to God.

Mortgage or rent payments: Having a roof over your head should be your first priority. Don't wait too long to analyze your housing situation if financial problems begin to occur. If you're renting your home and the rent payment is too high, move. If you wait too long, you may not be able to come up with the first month's rent plus the security deposit. Also, you want to have a good payment record with your current landlord.

If moving is not an option, contact your landlord immediately to explain your situation. See if he or she will work with you.

If you're buying your home and the mortgage payment is too high, look into refinancing your home to lower the payment. If refinancing isn't an option, sell the house. It would be better to sell the house and use the equity from the sale to move into a less expensive home rather than lose it through a foreclosure. You also risk a negative entry on your credit report, which can further hurt your chances in obtaining a new home loan for a purchase or refinance.

If you know you're going to be late in making your payment, contact your mortgage holder to see if they can assist you. Many lenders are willing to work out a new payment schedule. The last thing a lender wants to do is foreclose.

Utilities: Water, gas, electricity, and phone services are necessities. Cable television, Internet connection, and cell phones with all the bells and whistles are not.

Contact the utility company to make payment arrangements. When you get a late notice and a notice of disconnection, contact the company immediately. Many companies have special programs that are available to help people keep their utilities from being interrupted.

Food: Food is obviously a must and should be a priority. Even though it's not a debt, it's essential to survival and should be a first priority.

Vehicle payments: Transportation to and from work is a priority. If you have a car payment, try to stay current. If you know your payment will be late, contact the creditor. If your vehicle payment is too high, sell the vehicle. Use the money to get a vehicle by paying all cash or one with a lower monthly payment. See chapter 9 for more about handling a car loan.

Secured loans: A secured loan is one in which a particular item that is security or collateral for the loan will be returned to the creditor if your obligation is not met. Examples of secured items are your car, home, furniture, or boat—anything pledged as security. If you're having problems making the payment on a secured loan and it's not a necessity or survival item, sell it or return it. If it's an item you must have, make payment arrangements with the creditor. Late payments will also be reported on your credit report.

Medical insurance: Medical insurance is a must for most people; however, it can be quite costly. If you have a medical problem and your insurance lapses, you'll have problems getting insurance elsewhere. Contact your insurance carrier to see if there are other policies with a higher deductible that will reduce your monthly premium. Shop around for comparable insurance at a better rate, or perhaps you belong to an association such as a credit union or chamber of commerce that offers members group rates. Remember: a medical emergency without insurance can bankrupt you!

Child support: There's no excuse for not paying child support. For one thing, you can go to jail for that. A judgment may be filed against any individual who doesn't pay his or her child support. Wages may be garnished, and your failure to pay may be entered on your credit report. Child support cannot be discharged through a bankruptcy. Don't wait until further legal action is taken against you.

If your income has dropped, contact an attorney to see if you're eligible for a reduction, or contact the district attorney's office for assistance.

Property taxes: You must pay your property taxes each year. If you don't, a lien will be placed on your property, and the county can force a sale. It would be wise to set up an impound account with your mortgage company to add property taxes into your payment. If you don't have an impound account, calculate the amount due, divide it by twelve, and put that amount into a separate savings account every month so you have it when your property taxes are due.

Homeowner's insurance: All mortgage lenders require that you have homeowner's insurance. If you don't, the lender will provide its own at a much higher premium than a regular policy. If you have a hard time saving for the annual premium, you can also impound it with your mortgage payment. You can also set it up with your insurance company so that you can make monthly, quarterly, or annual payments.

Unpaid federal or state taxes: If you owe back taxes, the Internal Revenue Service or the state you owe can collect by garnishing your wages, attaching your bank accounts, and placing a lien on your home or other property.

Contact the IRS and state to make arrangements for repayment or to make an Offer in Compromise. An Offer in Compromise, if accepted, will reduce the amount that you owe. For example, say you owe $15,000 in back taxes. You can contact a tax relief company to help you negotiate with the IRS or do it yourself. You may offer $5,000 to settle the back taxes. The IRS will review your financial situation and determine if they'll accept your offer or come back with an amount they'll accept. Once the Offer in Compromise is accepted, you can make payments or pay the amount in full.

Whether you make a payment arrangement on your own or through an Offer in Compromise, stick to it, or the consequences may result in severe penalties, and the arrangement will be canceled, making the whole balance due in full.

Tithes: "Each man should give what he has decided in his heart to give, not reluctantly or under compulsion, for God loves a cheerful giver" (2 Corinthians 9:7).

Even when times are tough, God has a way of coming through when you're doing the right thing by paying your tithe. You're honoring God's Word. Blessings follow when you give from your heart.

CATEGORY 2: ESSENTIALS

Debts in the "essentials" category must be paid. However, they may have to be set aside for a time and paid at a later date. The consequences are not as severe in Category 2 as they are in Category 1, but there will be negative effects.

Credit cards bills: Most credit cards are unsecured, so if you fall behind in making your payments, nothing will be repossessed or taken from you. The creditor will make numerous attempts to collect the debt, but the worst that can happen is a negative entry on your credit report, your account will be closed, and the creditor may sue you.

Most creditors don't report a late payment on your credit report the first month you're late, but they'll report it if you don't make the second payment.

If you need a credit card for your business or personal use, select one card with the lowest interest, and pay the minimum amount due, on time, without fail.

If you keep one card because you need it for your home or business, move the payments on that card to Category 1. If you feel your interest rate is too high, call the credit card company and ask if the interest rate can be lowered. That's sometimes a possibility.

Department store and gasoline cards: Department store and gasoline charge cards are not secured. If you stop paying, you risk a lawsuit. They'll report a negative entry on your credit report.

If you keep one of your major credit cards active, such as Visa or MasterCard, use the card for your purchases. Pay the department store and gasoline charge cards when you can.

Keep in mind that late fees and interest will continue to mount. Many times the late fees push the credit card balance over the credit limit and cause an over-the-limit fee to be added to your balance. That puts you in the position of having to pay a late fee and an over-the-limit fee every month until the account balance is under the credit limit and is brought current. Those fees and penalties add up quickly and are not fun ways to spend your money.

Unsecured loans: Unsecured loans are usually loans made by a finance company, bank, savings and loan, or credit union. Failure to pay these could result in a negative credit report and a possible lawsuit.

Attorney, medical, and accounting bills: Pay attorney, medical, and accounting bills when you can set up a payment arrangement. Any one of these bills can be turned over to a collection agency, resulting in a negative entry on your credit report and a possible lawsuit.

CATEGORY 3: OTHER PRIORITIES

The following is a list of debts you may possibly have that also demand attention. Now is the time to move them to one of the other categories. By not paying an item listed below, you may or may not suffer severe consequences. You may have to put up with screaming creditors, however.

When completing your worksheet, place each of these in the appropriate category according to your specific situation.

Medical insurance: Some people feel that medical insurance is not a necessity—especially if they're healthy. We don't believe that's the best line of thinking. If you don't have medical insurance and you aren't sure if you or one of your family members is getting proper medical care, it's devastating. Even if you qualify for Medicare or Medicaid, a deductible may still be required.

If you drop medical insurance to save money and then are forced to face a medical emergency without it—as our family was when Melinda needed emergency brain surgery—your problems have multiplied.

If you or a family member has current medical problems and you let your insurance lapse, you may not be able to get insurance in the future because of the "preexisting condition." If you don't have any medical problems now and you let the policy lapse, you may be faced with something unforeseen. Carefully analyze the consequences of that happening and consider your options. Maybe you can reduce your premium by getting a higher deductible or going to catastrophic insurance.

In our opinion, medical insurance should be placed in Category 1.

Life insurance: Life insurance is usually the first thing to go during financial difficulties. It's important to consider age when considering whether or not to let life insurance lapse.

The older you are, the more difficult and more expensive it will be to get a good life insurance policy when your finances improve. You'll have to prove that you're healthy, and the premiums will be higher because of your age. If you really don't need life insurance because you have no dependents or your spouse is financially independent, this is a good place to reduce some of your debt.

If you can cash in your policy, you may be able to use the proceeds to pay off additional debt.

You must determine which of the first two categories life insurance should be in according to your situation.

Automobile insurance: As stated earlier, most states require automobile insurance. If you don't have it, you risk losing your drivers license as well as facing legal action if you're stopped by the police or have a car accident.

Check the requirements in your state. Contact your insurance agent to get the best possible rates, and maybe go to a higher deductible.

We think automobile insurance belongs in Category 1.

Childcare, private schools, and tutoring: If you work and have young children, childcare is an issue. It's important that children be taken care of properly. If you need childcare, check out all your options.

You may be able to co-op with other mothers to watch your children. Another possibility is to hire a babysitter to come to your home, which may cost you less than placing them in a daycare center.

Private schools or outside tutoring may be unnecessary, depending on whether or not your child has special needs. You may find it necessary to put your child in public school, which your tax dollars are already paying for, instead of college preparatory school. Evaluate whether or not the local public school system is adequate for your child's needs.

Gyms, spas, health clubs, and country clubs: Gyms, spas, health clubs, and country clubs are all luxuries. If you're having money trouble, these must go. Play golf at a public course; go for a walk with a friend. Use the money you save to reduce your debt.

Shopping: If you're having money trouble, you can't afford to be a slave to fashion. Skip the mall unless there's a spectacular sale going on. Think garage sale, yard sale, and clothing outlets. Surf the web for sites such as Ebay and discount stores. Watch the newspaper for sales. Children grow and need new clothes, but be smart in your purchases. Give up designer labels.

Personal services such as gardeners, a pool service, or someone to clean your house: Luxuries! You can do all or most of your domestic maintenance and cleaning yourself. If you really can't perform these services for yourself, cut back on the number of times you employ someone to do them.

Other: If you're making payments on anything that hasn't been covered, classify it and add it to the correct category on your worksheets.

Never make a payment on something from Category 2 unless you've made all your payments in Category 1. A roof over your head is the top priority, even if you can't pay anything on your credit cards. *Never* pay a credit card until you have paid the mortgage or rent, food, and utilities.

By following this plan, you will develop good paying habits, always taking care of your home and family first. Many creditors will intimidate you with rude telephone calls and letters. Be firm with your plan of repayment. Don't let a creditor bully you into making a payment you can't make without skimping on a Category 1 payment.

If you can't pay now, say that you'll pay when you can. Don't promise to pay something that you can't follow through with.

TOUGH-TIME TIPS

- Always pay essential survival bills such as mortgage or rent, food, and utilities first.
- The creditor who calls first or seems the most intimidating is not necessarily the one you should pay first.
- Don't make promises you can't keep.
- Complete your priority list each month.

Category 1 Worksheet: Survival

List your creditors and record the amount of the monthly payments. This category must be paid first.

Example:

Creditor	Monthly Payment
Rent or Mortgage	$1,200
Electric	$75
Gas	$32
Water	$40
Telephone	$35
Food	$250
Automobile	$300
Secured Loans	$120
Medical Insurance	$200
Unpaid Taxes	$50
Tithes	$100

Creditor	Monthly Payment
Rent or Mortgage	
Electric	
Gas	
Water	
Telephone	

Food	
Automobile	
Secured Loans	
Medical Insurance	
Unpaid Taxes	
Tithes	
Child Support	
Other	

Category 2 Worksheet: Essentials

List the creditors that are in this category, and record the amount of the monthly payments. This category must be paid only after those in Category 1 have been paid.

Example:

Creditor	Monthly Payment
Credit and Charge Cards	$160
Department Store Cards	$15
Gasoline Cards	$10
Unsecured Loans	$40
Attorney, Medical, Accounting	$50

Creditor	Monthly Payment
Credit and Charge Cards	
Department Store Cards	
Gasoline Cards	
Unsecured Loans	
Attorney, Medical, Accounting	
Other	

Category 3: Other Priorities Worksheet

List the creditor and the amount of the monthly payments. Every item on this list should be placed in one of the first two categories according to your situation—or eliminated altogether.

Example:

Creditor	Monthly Payment
Automobile Insurance	$150
Life Insurance	$50
Child Care, Private School, or Tutoring	$300
Club Memberships	$40
Clothing	$30

PAYMENT PRIORITIES

Creditor	Monthly Payment
Automobile Insurance	
Life Insurance	
Child Care, Private School, or Tutoring	
Club Memberships	
Clothing	
Medical Insurance	
Club Memberships	
Attorney Fees	
House Cleaner	
Gardner	
Pool Service	
Other	

12 BUDGET STRATEGIES THAT WORK

> Commit to the Lord whatever you do,
> and your plans will succeed.
> —Proverbs 16:3

Setting a budget is something that must be done prayerfully and honestly. Owning up to what you're spending is often a tough thing to do.

Most people cringe when they hear the word budget. However, without one, there's no way to get a grip on cash coming in and cash going out. In other words, you have to evaluate your spending habits. It's common for people to list the obvious bills and expenses but fail to include those "budget busters" such as frequent trips to the coffee shop or the fast food drive-through.

If you think setting up a budget is hard, sticking to it is even harder. It's time-consuming and sometimes painful. It takes discipline and accountability to stick to a budget. However, the benefits are rewarding, and you'll reach your financial goals much more quickly if you have something in writing to keep you on track. A budget becomes even more important if you're having money trouble.

CHANGING DIRECTION

Putting yourself on the right path may require you to change your outlook and your thinking about money and spending; and it may cause you some initial frustration as you change your behavior patterns. But it can be done!

A budget is just a tool to help you determine where your money is being spent. Rather than reacting to your expenses and your bills as they come in, a budget will help you allocate money for anticipated expenses. Once you've come up with a workable plan, it's easier to make adjustments and see where you're making mistakes. Wouldn't it be a relief to set money aside for things such as vacations, college, and retirement?

One key component to setting up a budget you can live with is honesty with yourself regarding your debts and everyday living expenses. You must also know how much you have coming in each month to pay your bills and what assets you have. Knowing these things will help you remain focused on the whole picture. If you're running short each and every month, a budget will help you figure out where you're spending needlessly and get to the bottom of why your indebtedness doesn't seem to be diminishing much.

Setting a yearly budget can be helpful if you're self-employed or paid on commission and don't know *exactly* how much you will bring in month to month.

A word of warning: As mentioned before, if you're self-employed or paid on commission, don't take the large amount of money you earn this month and spend it all, only to run short next month. Those once-in-a-while large checks can create a false sense of security. You need to determine what it takes for a year to run your household to pay your bills. Divide it by twelve. Anything that comes in over that amount in any given month should be set aside. This will eliminate falling behind when you have a slow month.

WRITE IT DOWN

One of the most important steps in building your budget and gaining control over your finances is to calculate your net worth. If you were to apply for a business loan, home loan, or automobile loan, you would complete an application that would give the potential lender an idea of your net worth. Net worth is calculated by taking your total assets and subtracting your total liabilities. Calculate it at the beginning of every year to see what progress you're making in accomplishing your financial goals.

Example

Net Worth Statement

Assets

Cash on Hand	$125
Checking Account	653
Savings Account	4,978
Money Markets	5,000
Accounts Receivable	11,740
Stocks & Bonds	15,000

Notes Receivable	3,430
Cash Value Life Insurance	25,000
Automobiles (Value)	22,700
Real Estate (Value)	98,000
Household Goods	9,700
Business	210,000
Inventory	10,000
Total Assets	**$406,326**

Liabilities

Real Estate Loan	$70,000
Automobile Loan	15,000
Student Loan	14,000
Credit Card Balances	9,890
Department Store Balances	764
Accounts Payable	4,200
Taxes Payable	2,900
Medical Expenses	1,000
Total Liabilities	**$117,754**

Total Assets minus Total Liabilities = **$288,572**

Net Worth Worksheet

Assets

Cash on Hand _____
Checking Account _____
Savings Account _____
Money Markets _____
Accounts Receivable _____
Stocks & Bonds _____
Notes Receivable _____
Cash Value Life Insurance _____
Automobiles (Value) _____
Real Estate (Value) _____

Household Goods _____
Business _____
Inventory _____
Other Assets _____
Total Assets _____

Liabilities

Real Estate Loan _____
Automobile Loan _____
Student Loan _____
Credit Card Balances _____
Department Store Balances _____
Accounts Payable _____
Taxes Payable _____
Medical Expenses _____
Other Liabilities _____
Total Liabilities _____

Total Assets minus Total Liabilities = _____ Net Worth

GEORGE AND MARIE'S STORY

George and Marie were losing ground with their finances—and fast. Marie worked part time, and George had a job that paid him on commission only. Some years George's annual income was quite high. Then there were the years that his income dropped off. There was no consistency.

The problem was that George and Marie were living as though they had a high income every year. They were reckless spenders. If you asked them where their money went, they couldn't tell you. They had become accustomed to a certain lifestyle and were unwilling to change it. But the day of reckoning eventually arrived.

They were unable to keep up with their monthly bills. George had cashed in his pension and 401K. He started getting cash advances from his credit cards to pay bills, resulting in maxed-out credit cards. The couple was drowning in debt.

After careful review, it was apparent they were just a step away from bankruptcy. They had three children living at home—all in private schools. One was about to start college. Drastic changes were required to avoid severe financial consequences.

The list of debts George and Marie prepared wasn't the whole picture. They had not included miscellaneous expenses or annual expenses, thus creating a false picture.

We advised them to write in a journal or log every dollar they spent for the next sixty days. At the end of thirty days they were to come together and categorize all expenditures and the amount spent. They would continue this procedure another thirty days to see where their money was going. This would give them a full sixty days to review and determine where they could cut back.

Since George was paid on commission, both he and Marie needed to prepare an annual budget to see how much money they needed to live on. The annual budget would help them establish a monthly budget. If George received a high commission check for one month that was more than they needed to exist, they were instructed to set that money aside to add to the following month commission. It was important that they stay two or three months ahead of their bills to keep from coming up short when they faced a month when commissions were low.

By setting a monthly budget and eliminating the excess money they had been spending—after the sixty-day review of their spending habits—George and Marie were in a better position to live within their means and know exactly where their money was being spent.

SETTING UP YOUR BUDGET

As we mentioned before, setting up a budget and adhering to it is not easy. It's often stressful, and it takes discipline and accountability—but the benefits are very rewarding.

BUDGET STRATEGIES THAT WORK

To determine your budget, write down all the debts and payments you make. Include everything—your living expenses too. Then make a list of the money you have coming in monthly. You must know exactly what you owe, what your payments are, and what income you have coming in on a monthly basis. If you have trouble doing this, look at your living expenses from the past year. This will help you calculate your general household costs. Review check registers and credit card statements for the amounts you've spent over the past year for things like—

- Rent or mortgage
- Food
- Utilities
- Transportation
- Childcare
- Insurance
- Medical expenses
- Miscellaneous (review worksheet for other suggestions.)

Whether you write it out on a piece of paper or an online computer software program, just be sure to list every single thing you spend money on.

THE BUDGET-BUSTERS

Remember that expenditures paid once a year, quarterly, or monthly must be added to your monthly budget.

Separate your monthly and yearly expenses into two categories. The budget-busters—expenses that are not paid monthly—fall into yearly expenditures, and most people forget to set money aside to pay these. Examples include property taxes, insurance premiums, car maintenance bills, and so on. If your property tax bill is $1,200 per year, divide the bill by 12. That means you must set aside $100 each month to pay that when it comes due. So add that to your monthly budget.

To avoid succumbing to budget-busters, you must save for these expenses so you'll have the money available when the bill comes due. It's a good idea to have a separate savings account to keep that money separate so you won't be tempted to spend it.

The following are some examples of expenses that can turn into budget-busters.

Housing
Property taxes
Homeowner's insurance
Security systems
Home repairs and maintenance
Maintenance agreements

Utilities
Waste management
Water or water softener

Automobiles
Insurance
Registration of vehicles
Maintenance and repairs

Medical
Insurance
Disability insurance
Doctor and dental visits
Orthodontists
Vision exam, contacts, eyeglasses
Health maintenance

Memberships & Subscriptions
Tithes and offerings
Organizations and clubs
Professional licenses
Sports
Warehouse clubs
Magazines

Schooling
Tuition
Books and supplies

Office
Office equipment maintenance
Clothing
Work clothes
School uniforms
Clothing for family members
Clothing for sports
Recreation
Recreational hobbies
Vacations
Music lessons
Pets
Pet maintenance and food
Training
Miscellaneous
Life insurance
Accountant
Taxes
Savings
Investments
Gifts (birthday, anniversary, and so on)
Holidays
Other

If you're not sure what you're spending, refer to your check registry and credit card statements for the past twelve months. This will allow you to know exactly how much you spend and where the money goes.

❈ ❈ ❈

From the budget-buster list determine what items you must pay throughout the year. If you have expenses that are not included on our sample list, add them.

Divide the total of those expenses by twelve. That's the amount you'll need to set aside each month to have the funds available when the bills come. You would also enter the monthly total on you monthly budget worksheet.

Non-monthly Expense Worksheet

Example:

Category	Item	Amount	Months Due
Housing	Property Tax	1,400	12 months
Automobiles	Auto Repair	800	2 months
Schooling	Books	515	1 month
Miscellaneous	Savings	200	3 months
Pets	Training	150	1 month

Total = $3,065 $3,065/12 months = $255.42

Non-Monthly Worksheet

Category	Item	Amount	Months Due

Monthly Budget Worksheet

Complete this worksheet to determine your income and expense totals.

Month_____

	Projections	Actual
Income		
Salaries	_____	_____
Wages if self-employed	_____	_____
Commissions	_____	_____
Dividends	_____	_____
Rental income	_____	_____
Child support	_____	_____
Alimony	_____	_____
Other	_____	_____
Total income	_____	_____
Fixed Expenses		
Mortgage/Rent/Housing	_____	_____
Utilities	_____	_____
Food	_____	_____
Alimony	_____	_____
Child support	_____	_____
Automobile payments	_____	_____
Clothing	_____	_____
Installment payments	_____	_____
Credit card payments	_____	_____
Insurance premiums	_____	_____
Medical/dental care	_____	_____
Education	_____	_____
Recreation	_____	_____
Taxes (federal, state, local)	_____	_____
Tithing/Giving	_____	_____
Budget-busters	_____	_____
Total fixed expenses	_____	_____

MONEY TROUBLE

Total available income _____ _____
   (Subtract from fixed expenses)

Total excess _____ _____

Total shortage _____ _____

Yearly Budget Worksheet

Annual income

	Projections	Actual
Income		
Salaries		
Wages if self-employed		
Commissions		
Dividends		
Rental income		
Child support		
Alimony		
Other		
Total income		
Fixed expenses		
Mortgage/Rent/Housing		
Utilities		
Food		
Alimony		
Child support		
Automobile payments		
Clothing		
Installment payments		
Credit card payments		
Insurance premiums		
Medical/dental care		
Education		

Recreation	_____	_____
Taxes (federal, state, local)	_____	_____
Tithing/Giving	_____	_____
Budget-busters	_____	_____
(non-monthly payments)		
Total fixed expenses	_____	_____
Total available income	_____	_____
(Subtract from fixed expenses)		
Total excess	_____	_____
Total shortage	_____	_____

YOUR RESULTS

How did you come out after completing your worksheets? Did you have extra money after your budget was completed, or did you have a shortage?

Compare the total of what you pay out with the total of what you bring in. Do you have enough money to cover the basic costs of your lifestyle? If it's too close for comfort or you come up short, you're overspending. Don't panic. In the following chapters we'll show you ways to save money and methods for getting out of debt so you can begin saving.

Experts say you should have at least $2,000 saved in an emergency fund—not credit cards, but an actual savings account that earns you interest. If $2,000 seems too much for you right now, start with less. But start. If you can save $166.67 a month, you will have saved over $2,000 in a year.

In addition, having three to six months living expenses set aside will bring you peace of mind. If you're a single-income family, save enough to cover living expenses for six months. If both spouses work, a three-month reserve is an adequate goal.

Following is a recommendation of the percentage of income that goes into each category of your budget.

Housing: 35 percent

Debt reduction: 15 percent

Travel: 15 percent

Other: 15 percent

Tithing: 10 percent

Savings: 10 percent

Whether you have extra money left over or no money at all left over, it's a good idea to analyze your budget. You may be able to make some cuts in one of these categories that will allow you to pay off outstanding debt, set aside money for savings, or invest in your retirement. A budget enables you to have an overall picture of your financial reality, and that allows you to decide where you want or need your money to go. You control the flow; the flow doesn't control you.

If some of the numbers are causing your head to spin, sit back and give yourself some time to adjust to these new perspectives. Maybe the clear picture you suddenly see of your finances shocks you. Remind yourself that budgeting is not meant to force you into some overly ascetic, deprived, joyless lifestyle. A budget empowers you by letting you know how much is coming in, how much is going out, and how much you can save for future needs. It can also help you stay focused during lean times. Remember: the goal is to live within your means. It's going to feel really good when you know your expenses are covered.

MOVING AHEAD

When your budget is under control, you can begin to save. Instead of spending more, your new mind-set will hopefully be to save more. Knowing you have money to cover your costs with something set aside for emergencies will allow you to enjoy your life more abundantly. Not only that, but you can also reach out and help others in distress. You won't constantly be worrying about making ends meet or dreading "what if" scenarios. Likewise, building genuine financial security will increase your sense of well-being. It's a great confidence-builder to know you're in control of your finances and your money is working for you.

Once you have a good understanding of your financial picture, you can tackle the obstacles that stand between you and financial freedom. Think about what you want your money to do for you, your family, and others. You may want to enlist the help of a financial advisor to help you reach your goals of everything from buying a new home, sending your children to college, or investing and planning for retirement.

Setbacks along the way may cause you to revisit your plan and maybe make adjustments. Don't give up. In a short amount of time, you'll see a difference in your finances and will be taking steps to financial security.

TOUGH-TIME TIPS

- Be aware of what money you have coming in, and don't be in denial about the amount of money that's going out.
- List your assets and liabilities.
- Don't forget the budget-busters.
- Strive to put away emergency savings to carry your household for three to six months.
- Don't let your cash flow control you; you control the cash flow.

13
PLUG THE CASH LEAK, AND INCREASE THE CASH FLOW

All hard work brings a profit,
but mere talk leads only to poverty.
—Proverbs 14:23

After completing your budget and getting a grip on how much you need each month—and how short you are on what you need—it's time to plug the cash leak and increase the cash flow. Don't just talk about it! Take action. By following the recommendations in this chapter, you can free up money. It may take some convincing, but we can show you how you can cut back on common expenses, including automobile, credit cards, utilities, entertainment, insurance, meals and beverages, and shopping.

The average household boasts five or six credit cards that carry outstanding balances totaling between $15,000 and $20,000. With that much charge power per household, it's no wonder so many families spend or owe more than they bring home.

If you've arrived at the day of reckoning in your finances, and your monthly debt is exceeding your monthly income, you'll benefit from getting on board with these money-saving tips.

HOUSING

Can you afford to live where you're living? If you're using more than thirty-five percent of your income on housing costs, it's time to consider moving to a cheaper residence, advertising for a roommate, or reducing costs in another category to recoup some of what you're spending.

ELECTRICITY, GAS, AND WATER

Can you take steps to lower these costs? Sometimes just a few simple alterations to your apartment or house can reduce heating and cooling expenses. Be conscious of turning off lights and appliances.

- By adjusting your thermostat just one degree when you run your furnace or air conditioner, you can save a significant amount on your next bill.
- Cut down on the amount of water you use. Don't let the faucet run while you brush your teeth, and take shorter showers.
- If you have a fireplace, burn wood to help heat your home.

TELEPHONE

Are you getting the best deal on your telephone service?

Are you taking advantage of lower long-distance rates by calling on evenings and weekends? Can you use e-mail or write letters to stay in touch instead of calling long-distance?

Many people are canceling their land lines and using only their cell phones. Compare prices to see if that works for you.

- Shop for long-distance carriers. A difference of one cent per minute really adds up if you make very many long-distance calls.
- If you have a land line and you don't have unlimited minutes on your cell phone, resist the urge to chat, and use your cell phone only for emergencies.
- Cancel call-waiting, three-way calling, and caller ID services from your telephone.

FOOD

Food and groceries are a necessity. Still, you can save hundreds of dollars by shopping at low-cost stores, by using coupons, and by avoiding convenience stores that normally charge significantly higher prices. Think carefully about what you buy. Prepackaged foods are more expensive than buying ingredients to make home-cooked meals. If time is a factor, trade off by making a few of your meals as well as buying some of the ready-made items. If there are certain items you use often and use a lot of, buy them in bulk.

- Stash a box of breakfast cereal at your office; if there's a refrigerator at work, keep some milk on hand.
- Brown-bagging your lunch can save a lot of money.
- Instead of buying your snacks from the vending machine at work, buy your snacks from the grocery store, and keep them at work. Put the money you save in the bank.

MEALS, BEVERAGES, AND OTHER LUXURIES

- Take your own soft drink to work instead of buying it from a vending machine. You're probably paying anywhere from seventy-five cents to a dollar to buy a drink from a vending machine. Bringing one from home will cost about twenty-five cents. If you're spending seventy-five cents once a day for soda, the difference adds up to $65 a year. If you're currently paying a dollar for a drink from the vending machine, the savings would be $130. That's figured on one soft drink per day.
- Coffee money. If you're going to a coffee house and paying $2 a day for a cup of coffee every weekday, that's $480 a year. Buy a thermos, and take coffee from home.
- Resist the urge to eat out a few times a month, and eat at home instead. Apply the savings to one of your bills. When you do eat out, share meals. Heaven knows the portions they serve in many restaurants could feed two people. Order water instead of other drinks. Put the saved money into one of your empty coffee cans!

AUTOMOBILE AND TRANSPORTATION EXPENSES

Most households spend fifteen percent of their income for automobile or other travel expenses. If you're spending more than that, there may be some ways you can cut back. Some companies have carpooling programs that pay you money to carpool with co-workers or take public transportation. Maybe you could bike or walk to work. Or maybe you can take a bus to work two days a week and drive the other days.

Are you getting the best gas prices? Are you taking good care of your vehicle with regular oil changes, tune-ups, and other routine maintenance? A vehicle is an investment, and in terms of the bigger financial picture, you can save money by making sure it runs well and hanging on to it for several years. If your vehicle is costing you money due to numerous repairs, you may want to look into buying another one.

- Buying a good used vehicle instead of a new one will save a lot of money.
- Pump your own gas instead of paying for full service.
- Before buying a different vehicle, find out how it will affect your auto insurance premium.

CHILDCARE

If you're paying for childcare and feel that you've found someone you trust or a program that works for your child, stay with it. You can save money elsewhere. If you're not satisfied with your current childcare situation, try to find a good deal while keeping your child's welfare in mind. If you're looking for an occasional day off from mom duty or you would like to have a date night, perhaps you can swap babysitting with a couple of close friends a few times a month.

- Home-schooled teenagers make great babysitters.
- A retiree may want to swap babysitting for having the grass mowed or other high-energy household tasks.
- Contact your church for help in locating a babysitter.

BANKING

- Review your business and personal checking account statements. Total the monthly service charges, plus all the additional charges you accumulate each time you make an ATM withdrawal from outside your bank's network or debit card transactions that incur fees from the merchants. That can amount to an additional $20-plus dollars per month.
- To eliminate these charges, find a bank that doesn't charge monthly service fees.
- Go only to ATMs affiliated with your bank so you don't have to pay a fee. This can save you $1 to $2 per transaction.

CREDIT CARDS

Review your credit card statements every month. You may be surprised by the number of errors. There may be charges you didn't make or unwarranted finance charges.

- Compare your monthly statement to your previous charges and receipts.
- Pay your credit card balances in full each month, and eliminate the finance charges and interest of ongoing balances.

ENTERTAINMENT

- Don't buy lottery tickets.
- Cut out cable television features you never or seldom use. Better yet, cut out cable altogether.
- Rent movies instead of going to the movie theater at $7 to $10 a person.
- Check out movies and books from the library. It's free!
- Go to matinees when ticket prices are reduced instead of going to the movies in the evening.

INSURANCE

- Review your medical coverage. See if you can save money by getting higher deductibles.
- Review your car insurance policy. Shop around for cheaper rates. Get higher deductibles.

MEDICAL INSURANCE

If you have medical insurance with a deductible, see if the medical provider will discount your out-of-pocket expenses.

- If you have no medical insurance, find out if the medical provider or facility will settle for the discounted amount an insurance company would pay.
- Negotiate with the health care provider. Many will discount the bill.

MEMBERSHIPS AND SUBSCRIPTIONS

- Drop your gym or health club membership. Invest in video workouts. Use a cinderblock to do your step aerobics, and use canned vegetables for weights. Remember the hula hoop? It really works!
- Get your news from radio or television instead of the newspaper.
- Don't renew your magazine subscriptions. Go to the library, or use the Internet.

SHOPPING

- When shopping for clothes or a major purchase, go home and sleep on it. This can curb impulse buying.
- Comparison shop. If there's an item you really need, check out the prices at other stores before you make the purchase.
- Clip coupons and shop at grocery stores that will double—or even triple—the coupon's value.
- Take advantage of rebates. If you buy a product that comes with a rebate offer, use it. Even if the amount seems low, money from rebates adds up quickly.
- Shop garage sales and secondhand stores for clothing and toys. Go to discount stores for terrific buys.

FUN MONEY-SAVER

Here's a fun way to save money while losing weight and inches. The following mini-chart will show you how the money you spend on little tasty luxuries, if saved instead, can make you money. And as a bonus, you can save calories!

This is taken from our book *Rich and Thin: Slim Down, Shrink Debt, & Turn Calories into Cash*, published by McGraw-Hill.

MONEY TROUBLE

Money Calorie-Counter

Based on 5 days a week   10% int. Compounded

Item	Cost	Calories	Monthly Calories	Yearly Calories	Monthly Cost	Yearly Cost	10 Yr. Savings	20 Yr .Savings
Donuts	.75	170	3683	44,200 (13 lbs.)	$16.25	$195.00	$3,318.49	$12,339.74
Hamburger	.95	270	5850	70,200 (20 lbs.)	20.58	247.00	$4,215.71	$15,627.81
Fries	lg. 2.05	540	11,700	140,400 (40lbs.)	44.42	533.00	$9.099.21	$33,731.16
Pizza 1 slice cheese	2.50	309	6695	80,340 (23 lbs.)	54.17	650.00	$11,696.45	$41,135.00
Mocha Latte 16 oz.	3.05	270	5,859	70,200 (20 lbs.)	66.08	793.00	$13,536.16	$50,179.09
Chocolate Candy Bar Lg.	.89	510	11,050	132,600 (38 lbs.)	19.28	231.40	$ 3,949.41	$14,640.63

BARTERING

Bartering is the art of exchanging one commodity or service for another. If you can trade a skill, service, or item for something in return, do it. Bartering is a win-win situation for both parties and doesn't cost money.

TRACY AND NANCY'S STORY

Tracy loves a hot cup of coffee. Every morning she and a coworker, Nancy, visit a specialty coffee shop near their office. Tracy buys a cup of gourmet coffee for $1.50, and Nancy orders a latté for $2.75. At the end of the week, Tracy has spent $7.50 for her coffee, and Nancy has spent $13.75. On a monthly basis, Tracy spends $30, and Nancy puts out $55. Calculated yearly, respectively, it comes to $360 and $660.

Both Tracy and Nancy could save money by altering their coffee habits. Brewing their coffee at home and bringing it to work in a travel thermos could greatly lower their costs. Possibly once a week—say on Fridays—the two could go to their coffee shop and treat themselves to their favorite selections.

ADDING IT UP

The preceding examples illustrate how looking at the true cost of a seemingly small luxury really adds up. This is one of those instances where tracking your spending quickly reveals a cash drain.

Hopefully these examples also show you that with a little creative ingenuity you can still enjoy your treat and save some money. Here are some other tips you might want to consider to help pull back on discretionary spending:

- Know what you need, make a list, and shop only from that list. This applies to clothes, food, and household items.
- Shop for clothes and shoes on sale or off-season.
- Buy items that are classics rather than fads that will quickly go out of style.
- Avoid purchasing items that require dry cleaning.
- Buy cosmetics at the drugstore rather than the department store; no one will know if you paid $5 or $25 for your lipstick.
- Do your own manicures and pedicures.
- Set a gift budget, and stick to it. Or try offering a personal service or some other small but thoughtful gesture.
- Make sure vacations are paid for and not bought on credit with the idea of paying later.
- When making travel arrangements, look for airfare bargains as well as off-season rates and special discounts.
- Get a library card, and check out books, videos, and CDs for free; you can also catch up on most of the latest magazines at your local library.
- Swap services with a friend.
- Try repairing items instead of replacing them.

Getting real about finances may seem like a nightmare at first. You may feel depressed, anxious, overwhelmed, and unable to wrap your mind around the fact that a few dollars saved here and there can really make much difference. Maybe you're shocked at the amount of cash that slips through your fingers for little things you hardly notice, and you're kicking yourself for letting that money get away from you. Remind yourself that while you can't change yesterday, you can start making changes today. Be patient with yourself and with your new budget. New habits take time.

Often people think that tracking their expenses, especially the small day-to-day costs, is a waste of time. They think it's too hard to carry a notepad around and jot down every dime and dollar. Besides, how much difference will a couple of dollars and a little loose change make? Part of the reason we ask clients to track their expenses is to show them that all those little expenditures add up. That's why it's important to track expenses for at least thirty days. That helps you get a good sense of what you're spending on incidentals. Add credit cards to the mix for a more complete picture of your spending habits. It will also help you identify where you can cut back and make adjustments. If you're one-half of a married couple, double the expenditures and potential savings. When you keep your expense log, jot down the details of what you're spending. Don't just pass the cost off as a miscellaneous item.

ATMS AND DEBIT CARDS, AKA MONEY THIEVES

Most people who use ATMs or debit cards have difficulty tracking their spending. If you aren't realistic about your use of these, you'll have a hard time sticking to a budget.

There are two ways to save on your ATM withdrawals. One way is to make sure you use only ATMs that won't charge you a fee. Hardly anyone remembers to add those fees to the budget.

If you visit machines that are not affiliated with your bank, you can pay $4 or more in fees on just one transaction. Do this five times a month, and you've added $20 to your budget.

The second approach is to budget for your anticipated daily cash expenses and take out only that amount each week. Every time you take money from the ATM, write it down in your notepad, and list what you'll spend the money on. Don't just take out $20 and not account for it. List how you spent each penny of that withdrawal. This will help you see where your ATM money goes. Most people have no idea what they spend these withdrawals on, even though they note the withdrawal transaction in their check ledger. Don't make the mistake of spending whatever is in your account each month until it's gone. Begin exercising control over you money and spending.

BREAKING OLD HABITS

Breaking old habits and establishing new ones takes time. If you slip up, keep working on it. An awareness of the problem generally helps keep you on track. It won't be easy at first, but be persistent. Maybe it will help you stay motivated to keep a note on your refrigerator reminding you of how much you saved in a week. Believe in yourself. God will give you strength and perseverance. "I can do all things through Christ who strengthens me" (Phillipians 4:13, NKJV).

YOUR CASH AND CREDIT CARD JOURNAL

To help you track your day-to-day expenditures, make a list of purchase categories—dining out, fast food, clothing, coffee, toiletries, gasoline, magazines, CDs, movies, prescriptions, personal toiletries—in your journal or notepad. Then list what you spend in the applicable category. At the end of thirty days, total what you spent in each category, and then add up all the categories for a grand total. Shocked?

Tracking Your Cash Expenditures

Example

Use the following worksheet as a guide to keeping a list of your cash expenditures for thirty days. Write down everything! At the end of thirty days, total each category separately, and add up all the categories.

Date	Meals	Fast Food	Clothing	Personal
Month & day		$5.75	$32.17	$6.75

MONEY TROUBLE

_____

_____

_____

Totals _____

Tracking Your Credit Card Expenditures

Log all your credit card transactions for thirty days. Write down each expense, and separate these expenses by categories. Get in the habit of saving your receipts and comparing them with your monthly credit card statement.

Date	Merchant	Meals	Clothing	Gasoline

Extra Cash Worksheet

Create a list of ways you can cut back, and apply the extra money toward your bills or savings. Enter the dates, items you saved money on, and the amount you saved. Don't forget to set the savings aside to put into a special fund. Do this daily.

PLUG THE CASH LEAK

Example

Date	Item	Cost	Amount Saved
9/14/XX	Soda		.35
9/14/XX	Coffee		1.75
9/14/XX	Meal		9.00
		Total Savings	

Extra Cash Worksheet

Date	Item	Cost	Amount Saved
		Total Savings	

Goals

Keep a list of the money you've saved over the past thirty days. Allow yourself to feel good about your new habits. Then make a list of all the things you can do with that saved money—maybe pay down bills or grow your savings. Think of something you would like to save for, and then put your money toward that goal. Enjoy the fruits of your penny-pinching efforts.

MONEY TROUBLE

Date	Item	Money Saved	Money Goals

TOUGH-TIME TIPS

- Carry a journal or notepad to use in tracking all your expenditures.
- Consciously watch for ways you can save money.
- Put the money you save into a special account to help you reach your financial goals.

14
GET OUT AND STAY OUT—OF DEBT

The rich rule over the poor, and the borrower is servant to the lender.
—Proverbs 22:7

Now that you have ways to live within your means and control your finances, it's time pull your plan together and pay off your debt—once and for all. This is not an overnight process, but it will be rewarding as each debt is paid off. God will give you strength and discipline.

As you analyze your situation, it may seem overwhelming, as if you can't see light at the end of the tunnel. Just remember the scripture that says, "I can do everything through him who gives me strength" (Philippians 4:13). You may need to repeat that often as you work through the financial maze.

STRATEGIES THAT WORK

Getting out of debt is a lot harder than getting in. You'll be discouraged at times, and you'll have to exercise discipline and perseverance. The Scriptures talk about trials and tribulations we have to face, and whether or not you're facing a financial crisis right now, debt feels like a noose around your neck. Getting out from under the burden of indebtedness is like having a heavy weight lifted from your shoulders.

There are several strategies to becoming debt-free; one of them will fit your situation.

Let's start with credit cards. Most people have no idea what credit card use really costs. Here's a quick quiz to see how much you really know about your credit cards.

Memory Quiz

Without looking at your statements, what are your current balances, credit limits, payments, and interest rates on each of your credit cards?

Complete the following Memory Debt Worksheet. Once you've completed it, do the second worksheet, listing all the accounts and information from your recent credit card statements.

Memory Debt Worksheet

Creditor   Balance   Credit Limit   Minimum Payment   Interest Rate

Reality Debt Worksheet

(Take the information from your credit card statements.)

Creditor   Balance   Credit Limit   Minimum Payment   Interest Rate

How did you do? Compare the two worksheets. Keep the Reality Debt Worksheet with your credit card statement information on it handy, because you'll be using it as a reference point for getting out of debt.

Most people don't read the details on the credit card statement that arrives each month. You know—the one with all those inserts you throw away. Most of the time those inserts contain messages from the credit card company that affect the terms of your agreement. It's those inserts that indicate changes to your interest rates. Many people look at the payment due and maybe the balance, but that's all. They're way more concerned about the amount of the payment than they are the interest rate they're being charged. If you don't pay attention to what you're paying in interest, you'll likely prolong the life of the debt. This is especially true if you're making only minimum monthly payments.

EXTRA PAYMENTS

Most of us don't calculate the length of time it takes to pay off credit card debt or how much is actually paid in interest before the debt is paid off.

One really good way to reduce your principal quickly is to pay more money than the minimum payment. By adding an extra $5, $10, or more to your monthly credit card payment, your debt will be paid more quickly, and you'll save a large amount in interest charges.

The average household carries at least five credit cards—and they all have balances. Every dollar you pay over the minimum required will allow you to pay your debt off quicker.

CONSOLIDATE YOUR CREDIT CARDS

After you've reviewed your Reality Debt Worksheet, you may feel that moving the balances of credit cards that charge higher interest rates to cards that charge lower rates would be in your best interest. This is a good idea if you've accepted credit cards with a zero-percent interest rate or another very low rate. *Be sure you know the details of these low teaser rates and when they will increase.* Also you need to know if there's a fee to transfer the balances to the lower-rate card. If it will save you money, even with a transfer fee, do it.

If you don't have a zero-percent interest rate, it will still benefit you to transfer balances on higher-rate cards to cards with lower rates. You'll be able to pay off the debt more rapidly and save money because of the savings on interest. The key to making this work to your advantage is that you *do not charge anything else on the higher-rate account!*

Department store credit cards should be consolidated to a Visa card or MasterCard with a lower interest rate. Department store cards usually charge higher rates of at least twenty-one percent, and some charge even higher rates. Close the account after you transfer the balance.

Example A

Credit Limit	Interest Rate	Current Balance	Minimum Payment
$5,000	16%	$1,200	$24
$2,000	21%	$1,800	$36
$1,000	22%	$500	$15

Example B—after first credit card balance transfer

Credit Limit	Interest Rate	Current Balance	Minimum Payment
$5,000	16%	$1,700	$39
$2,000	21%	$1,800	$36
$1,000	22%	$0	$0

Example C—after second credit card balance transfer

Credit Limit	Interest Rate	Current Balance	Minimum Payment
$5,000	16%	$3,500	$75
$2,000	21%	$0	$0
$1,000	22%	$0	$0

Notice that if you move the minimum payments and balances from each of the credit cards, you'll make one larger payment at a lower interest, allowing you to pay off the debt faster and save

MONEY TROUBLE

money on interest. Always try to pay more than the minimum payment every month.

USING THE SNOWBALL EFFECT TO YOUR ADVANTAGE

After reviewing your worksheet, prioritize each credit card from the highest credit card balance to the lowest credit card balance. For example:

APP Company	Balance: $2,300
NFX Company	1,200
Beta Credit Card	1,000
Department Store	500
Department Store	275

Experts have differing opinions about which card you should pay off first. Some think you should pay off high-interest/high-balance cards first, and others are convinced you should pay off high-interest/low-balance cards first. That's up to you, but the quickest way to get out of debt and feel that you're accomplishing something is to pay off the lower balances first. Then take the money you've been paying on the lowest balance, and add it to the next credit card balance. For instance, the balance of $275 had a payment of $15. Once that's paid, add the $15 to the next balance of $500 and so on until it's paid off. Then take the two payments you were making on the department stores, and add them to the next balance in addition to the minimum payment. These extra payments will apply to the principal and cause the balances to decrease rapidly.

Payoff Strategy Worksheet

Example: (Based on allocated amount of $500 per month)

Month	Creditor	Balance	Minimum Payment	Amount Paid
Month #1				
	APP Company	$2,300	$40	$45
	NFX Company	$1,200	$19	$25

GET OUT AND STAY OUT—OF DEBT

	Beta Credit	$1,000	$20	$250
	Dept. Store	$5,000	$10	$130
	Dept. Store	$275	$10	$275
Month #2				
	APP Company	$2,255	$40	$45
	NFX Company	$1,175	$19	$25
	Beta Credit	$975	$20	$60
	Dept. Store	$370	$10	$370
	Dept. Store	$0	0	0
Month #3				
	APP Company	$2,210	$40	$45
	NFX Company	$1,150	$19	$25
	Beta Credit	$915	$15	$430
	Dept. Store	0	0	0
	Dept. Store	0	0	0

Payoff Strategy Worksheet

Month	Creditor	Balance	Minimum Payment	Amount Paid

YOU WON'T GET A REDUCED RATE IF YOU DON'T ASK

A simple way to get a reduction of your interest rate with your credit card is to contact the credit company directly and ask for it. Tell them if you're being solicited by other credit card companies.

Many times if you ask, the credit card company will reduce the rate, but they won't do it on their own. So it's important that you make the call.

If they agree to lower the rate, be sure to continue making the higher payment so that more money is being applied to your principal.

DON'T REDUCE YOUR YEARLY ESTIMATED PAYMENTS

Review your yearly expenditures to see how much you were paying on your credit cards. Total the credit card payments, and divide that amount by twelve. As your balances decrease, your minimum payments will decrease. Use the amount that you estimated to pay for the year and continue paying the balances down. Pay the highest amount you can pay rather than the minimum.

EQUITY LOANS AND REFINANCING OPTIONS

Don't refinance your mortgage unless the payment is lower than you're paying now. Refinance only to a loan with a lower interest rate or to consolidate your bills. If it's to consolidate your bills, it's important that your monthly mortgage payment be lower than the total of the payments you're making on your bills. For example, if your mortgage is $1,000 per month and you have credit card bills totaling $500 per month, that would total $1,500. If your total payment after the refinance is $1,200, you've saved $300. A lender will evaluate your situation by calculating the ratio of your monthly income to your new payment minus your debts. If the ratio is between twenty-five and thirty-eight percent, you'll probably qualify for the new loan.

If it looks as if your bills will be paid off within a three-year period without refinancing the house, don't refinance. Refinancing should be done only if you're going to come out with a lower amount of money going out every month and if you're willing to discipline yourself by breaking the bondage of credit card use.

A refinance can cost thousands of dollars in loan fees and charges, plus it extends the life of your loan. New mortgages could be for fifteen, twenty, or thirty years.

A home equity loan is also known as a second mortgage. It could be set up as a fixed rate for fifteen, twenty, or twenty-five years, or set up as an equity line in which you're approved for a certain amount of money that equals the amount of equity you have in your home and you withdraw the money as you need it. For example, you may have an equity line of $50,000. You may need to withdraw only $15,000 for improvements or to pay off credit cards. You can use the money however you want. The equity line works like a credit card. The danger is that it can be perceived as easy money. An equity line without a fixed interest rate or set number of years is not our first choice, because most of the equity lines don't have a fixed interest rate. The interest rate is usually lower for the first three months of the equity line and adjusts to a much higher interest rate that causes the payment to be more than the consumer expected.

If you're late making the payments for your equity line, you risk losing your home through foreclosure, just as you would with your primary mortgage.

To refinance your property or get a second mortgage, you must have equity in the property.

People tap into their lines of credit for various reasons. Once that equity is used up, you can't tap into it again. As the principal balance decreases, you can tap into it as long as you don't exceed the credit limit.

With changes in the market, lenders can freeze the line of credit at any time and not allow you to draw on it. For example, if your equity line of credit was $100,000, and you used only $50,000, the lender can freeze the account not to exceed the $50,000. That has happened to many people in the past when there was a downturn in the housing market. More and more lenders felt the squeeze from borrowers withdrawing money and increasing their mortgages as the value of the property was decreasing. These people ended up owing more on their houses than the houses were worth and defaulted on their loans.

REVERSE MORTGAGES FOR SENIORS

More and more senior citizens sixty-two years of age and older are finding themselves short of money to pay their bills. If they're homeowners, a reverse mortgage may provide needed cash and a cushion for emergencies, repairs, medical needs, or other necessities. The benefit of a reverse mortgage is that the senior never has to make payments on the loan unless he or she wants to. See chapter seven for more information regarding reverse mortgages.

PAYING OFF THE MORTGAGE EARLY

You can reduce the life of your mortgage by adding additional money to your house payment each month. Setting up a bi-weekly payment schedule will also reduce years from your loan. The bi-weekly payment equates to one extra payment or more a year and can save hundreds of thousands of dollars for the life of your loan and shorten a thirty-year loan to approximately twenty-three years, but you must be consistent with the payments.

Visit <www.mortgage-x.com> to calculate the savings on your loan by paying it bi-weekly.

You can create the same effect by dividing your monthly payment by twelve months. For example, if your payment is $1,200 per month, and you divided the payment by twelve months, it would total $100 per month. Add an extra $100 every month to go to principal, and it will have the same effect of the biweekly payment—totaling one extra payment per year.

When your credit cards are paid off, add extra payments to your house payment. If you do this, write a note to your lender to apply the extra amount to the principal of your loan; you can generally note this on your monthly mortgage payment stub.

CREDIT AND DEBT MANAGEMENT COUNSELORS

You should consider contacting a credit counseling company to consolidate your debt whether you're delinquent in your payments, overextended with your credit cards, or just tired of paying high interest rates.

Credit counselors are known for the ability to rebuild consumers' relationships with their creditors. They become the middle party in communicating with your creditors. They can help work out your problems and develop a repayment program that will satisfy both you and those you owe.

When you contact a credit counselor, be ready with a list of your creditors' names, the balances you owe, and payments due. Also have information regarding your income and living expenses available. The counselor will look at your income, assets, debts, and expenses to determine what you can afford to pay.

If you've received any late notices, demand notices for payment, collection notices, notice of legal suits, court judgments, or anything you feel is significant for the counselor to review, have it ready to give to him or her. The counselor needs to see the whole picture in order to develop a payment plan that will help you and satisfy the creditors.

Once the counselor receives all the required information from you regarding your financial situation, he or she will contact your creditors to work out a repayment schedule.

As mentioned earlier, most creditors are eager to work with a credit counseling service, because they know that you're seriously seeking help and not filing for bankruptcy. They know that if you file for bankruptcy, they'll be unable to collect the debt, and that makes working with your credit counselor very appealing.

The credit counselor works with the creditor to lower the payment by reducing the interest to as low as zero or as high as eleven percent. Each creditor uses its own formula to determine the lower rate.

By reducing your interest rates, your total payment will be less than the total of what you're paying now. More of the new payment will apply toward principal, and that will allow you to pay off your debts in a shorter amount of time. You'll save thousands of dollars in interest and be debt-free. Your late fees and over-the-limit fees stop accruing when you work with a credit counseling company. If you've fallen behind on some of your bills, the accounts will be re-aged and brought current.

The credit counseling company will set your payments so that you're paying one monthly payment to the counseling service to cover all your debts. The counseling service will disburse your one payment to the creditors. You'll know exactly how much you'll be spending on debt reduction every month, and you'll know the principal balances are going down.

Don't wait until you're in deeper trouble to seek help. It's never too late. If you suspect you're overextended, are anticipating a job layoff or a divorce, have a disability, or are experiencing a reduction of income, get help right away.

SAVINGS ACCOUNT WITHDRAWALS

Clients often ask us if they should use their savings to pay off debts. If the money you have in savings is earning six-percent interest, and you're paying eighteen percent interest or more on your debts, you're losing money. Keep a small amount in your savings account for a rainy day, but use the remaining money to pay down your debt.

401K WITHDRAWALS

If you have a 401K account, you may be able to borrow against it, but you'll be required to pay that money back in monthly installments. If you simply withdraw money from your 401K, you'll have to pay taxes on it. Some 401K accounts are restricted by the employer so that employees can withdraw funds only for an emergency, such as a medical need. If you think this is an option, you should consult your financial adviser as to possible consequences. It's best not to touch your 401K and to leave it for your retirement.

BANKRUPTCY

Before considering bankruptcy, make sure you've consulted a credit counseling or debt management company. They may be able to find a better alternative. Bankruptcy laws have changed, making it more difficult. If you're considering bankruptcy, you should consult an attorney to see if you qualify, and if you file bankruptcy, credit counseling is mandatory.

Bankruptcy should always be the last resort. A bankruptcy will follow you for ten years on your credit report. If an employer is considering hiring you and runs a credit report listing the bankruptcy, you may not get the job. It will take you several years to rebuild your credit. If you're in the market for a home, mortgage, credit card, or automobile, you'll be charged higher interest rates.

For some people, however, bankruptcy is the right choice. Ask yourself if you can live with the consequences, and don't file for a bankruptcy just because you're tired of hearing from your creditors, and don't let a creditor bully you into bankruptcy.

A Chapter 7 bankruptcy is what's known as a straight bankruptcy. Filing Chapter 7 will make most of the debts disappear.

There are debts you can't discharge through a bankruptcy, however. Among them are student loans, overdue taxes, alimony, child support, or a loan you obtained fraudulently. A loan would be determined fraudulent if you exaggerated your income or other information on your loan application and the creditor is able to prove it. Charging up purchases before filing for bankruptcy can also be viewed as fraudulent. A creditor will take notice of purchases you made in the months leading up to your filing.

If you file for bankruptcy, it's advisable to have an attorney represent you. It's very risky to do it yourself. There are things you may omit or not fully understand on your own.

Once you've filed for bankruptcy, you must go to a meeting with the trustee (the person in charge of your bankruptcy). The trustee will determine what assets you have that can be sold to pay off the creditors. Also, the trustee will determine what debts you have that will be discharged through the bankruptcy. Dischargeable debts disappear after the bankruptcy, meaning you don't have to pay the debt off. These dischargeable debts include most unsecured debts, such as credit cards, medical bills, collection accounts, judgments, and rent.

A Chapter 13 bankruptcy is known as the federal repayment plan or wage earner plan. With the changes of the bankruptcy laws, most people are put into the Chapter 13 program, and it's less difficult to qualify for.

A Chapter 13 bankruptcy allows you to keep your property, and the court assigns a trustee to determine how much you should pay per month to settle the debts. If you file for Chapter 13, you will be required to submit a detailed budget of what your living expenses and bills total. You then will propose an amount that you can pay per month to the trustee who will disburse to the creditors. All interest charges and late fees are stopped.

If the court approves your payment proposal, you'll begin making payments. At the end of the term—based on what the court agrees to—any amount still owed on the debt is forgiven by the court, and no more payments are required.

The main difference between a Chapter 7 bankruptcy and a Chapter 13 is that the Chapter 7 wipes out most debts without repayment. Chapter 13 allows you to keep secured items such as your cars, home, or furniture by lowering your payments.

To qualify for a Chapter 13, you must be employed and earn enough money to meet your budgeted living expenses plus the payments you agree to pay by the court trustee. If you're unable to keep your payment arrangements in the Chapter 13, you may be eligible to file a Chapter 7 to discharge your debts and eliminate all your payments.

Both a Chapter 7 and Chapter 13 will appear on your credit reports for up to ten years from the discharge date.

SUPPORT OF FAMILY AND FRIENDS

If you borrow money from your family or friends, don't use the money to pay credit card bills or anything that's nonessential. Use that money for survival, such as mortgage or rent payments, food, and utilities. If you use the money for other things, you run the risk of falling behind with the basics, such as a place to live, utilities, or feeding your family.

Sometimes when a family member or friend volunteers financial help, it's not the best option. You'll feel obligated and uncomfortable if you can't pay it back sooner rather than later. If you do borrow money, sign a promissory note agreeing to pay the person back when you have the funds. Many relationships have been destroyed because of money.

Again, the most obnoxious bill collector is not necessarily the one to pay first. Keeping a roof over your head and food on the table is your first priority.

Don't use your family or friends as a crutch. If it's a dire emergency, accept their help. But don't get in the habit of accepting money from family or friends unless it's a true emergency. There needs to come a point when you find other remedies to solve your financial problems.

YOU CAN DO IT!

"Consider it pure joy, my brothers, whenever you face trials of many kinds, because you know that the testing of your faith develops perseverance. Perseverance must finish its work so that you may be mature and complete, not lacking anything" (James 1:2-4). There have been many times in our personal lives when we've clung to this scripture. It's hard to make such sweeping changes and become disciplined in our spending. It is worth it! What you will gain by achieving victory in your financial life is peace and joy, knowing that you can use some of your extra money to sow back to those in need.

TOUGH-TIME TIPS

- Add extra money to your minimum credit card payments.
- Contact your credit card company and ask for your interest rate to be reduced.
- Determine what you can pay each month on credit card debt, and keep it going until all your debts are paid in full.
- Never refinance or take a home equity line of credit if the balances on your debts can be paid off within three years.
- Add extra payments to your mortgage.
- Contact a credit counseling or debt management company if you're overextended or have fallen behind in making your payments. They will be able to negotiate lower payments for you.

15
PROTECT YOURSELF FROM IDENTITY THEFT

If any of you lacks wisdom, he should ask God, who gives generously to all without finding fault, and it will be given to him.
—James 1:5

Every year thousands of people become victims of identity theft. Dictionary.com defines identity theft as "the stealing of a person's financial information, especially credit cards and Social Security number, with the intention of using that data to commit fraud and create a phony persona." Identity theft can cause problems for the victim for years to come. It's important to understand how thieves steal personal information so you can take the appropriate steps to protect yourself.

MATT AND EMILY'S STORY

Matt and Emily were living paycheck to paycheck, because Matt had recently switched careers and had taken a large cut in pay. They often juggled bills until Matt got paid. They were shocked to discover, one day after depositing a paycheck, that their checking account had been emptied by an identity thief. Matt and Emily discovered the theft when they attempted to pay for lunch with their debit card and it was denied. They immediately called the bank and found out that they were overdrawn. There had been multiple charges made online that had completely drained the account. The bank reimbursed Matt and Emily, but it took several days. The identity thief had gotten their debit card information when they had used it at a restaurant several weeks earlier.

Identity theft has grown exponentially over the years with the advancement of technology. Unscrupulous individuals are able to find ways to obtain your most valuable and personal information. Under the Identity Theft and Assumption Deterrence Act of 1998, identity theft is considered a crime. When this law was enacted, it strengthened the criminal laws governing identity theft and provided a centralized consumer complaint process for its victims. According to the law (3.18 U.S.C. § 1028(a)(7)), it's a crime to "knowingly transfer or use, without lawful authority, a means of identification of another person with the intent to commit, or to aid or abet, any unlawful activity that constitutes a violation of

Federal law, or that constitutes a felony under any applicable state or local law."

There are many ways for the thieves to use information they steal. Credit card numbers can be used to make purchases, or your Social Security number can be used to open new lines of credit in your name. An identity thief may use your personal information to open a bank account and then write fraudulent checks that bounce. The thief might even get a driver's license in your name but with his or her own picture. The ways in which thieves use a stolen identity are endless, and it's challenging to recover if your identity is stolen.

HOW THEY GET YOUR INFORMATION

Identity thieves use many strategies to obtain personal information, and their tactics are continuously changing. Following is a list of common tactics.

Dumpster-diving: Believe it or not, thieves rummage through the garbage. They know that many consumers throw away documents with valuable information, such as credit card numbers, bank account numbers, and Social Security numbers. Identity thieves look for financial statements, old credit cards, checks, and any other documents that contain your information.

Stolen mail: An individual's mailbox is a goldmine for identity thieves. It's full of confidential data. Identity thieves use credit card and bank statements, tax information, and even those pre-approved credit offers.

Skimming: The term *skimming* is a way in which identity thieves use data storage devices to steal credit or debit card information. These devices are placed in areas that consumers frequently use their credit or debit cards, such as gas stations. When the card is swiped, the information is captured in the device and later used by the identity thief.

Businesses: Identity thieves are notorious for obtaining customer information from businesses by stealing records that contain confidential customer data. Sometimes these thieves are the employees of the business.

A lost or stolen wallet or purse: A wallet or purse has just about everything a thief needs to steal someone's identity—especially if it contains a Social Security card.

E-mail or telephone: Identity thieves contact persons via e-mail or the telephone posing as a representative from a real or fictitious company. They may ask the victim to verify his or her Social Security number or account number for some made-up reason. This type of identity theft is known as *phishing* or *pretexting*. Even if the person claims to represent a legitimate company you've heard of or done business with, be wary.

PROTECT YOURSELF

You can take proactive steps to avoid becoming a victim of identity theft. If in doubt, err on the side of caution.

Order a copy of your credit report at least once a year. This is one of the most important things you can do to prevent identity theft. By ordering a copy of your credit report, you can closely monitor the activity of your accounts. You should be in the habit of ordering your report from each of the three credit reporting agencies, TransUnion, Equifax, and Experian, once a year. The next chapter gives you information on how to obtain your credit report.

Check your mail often. Don't leave mail in your mailbox, and get into the habit of checking your mail on a daily basis. If your mailbox does not have a lock, consider sending and receiving your bills at the post office instead of leaving them in your mailbox.

Protect your computer. Hackers are experts at accessing private information on computers. If you have an "always on" Internet connection or use a wireless router, use a firewall, and don't store financial information on your hard drive. Wireless routers allow you to set up a password so only individuals who know the password can access your network.

Shred unneeded financial documents. Use a shredder when discarding financial documents such as credit card statements, bank statements, tax information, and pre-approved offers. Thieves retrieve a lot of information by going through trash. To cut down on the number of pre-approved credit offers you receive in the mail, call 888-567-8688 to opt out of telemarketing lists used by the credit reporting agencies.

Don't carry your Social Security card with you. If you lose your wallet or it's stolen, your Social Security number could be used to steal your identity.

Invest in a safe or filing cabinet with a lock. Store your personal documents such as Social Security cards, tax information, and credit card and bank statements in a secure area.

Keep a record in a safe place of the credit cards you carry. Use a note card to list credit cards you keep in your wallet so that if your wallet is lost or stolen, you'll know how to contact the company to report the lost or stolen card. You can use the My Financial Institutions worksheet at the end of this chapter to create that list.

IF YOU BECOME A VICTIM

Maybe you have already experienced identity theft firsthand and wonder how to overcome it. The following advice will help you.

RYAN AND CLARICE'S STORY

Ryan and Clarice were unaware that someone had stolen their personal information and opened a line of credit. The thief ran up a balance of approximately $50,000. The bank eventually came after Ryan and Clarice to collect the delinquent payments and to pursue a judgment against them. The bank had sent numerous letters regarding the debt, but Ryan and Clarice had disregarded the letters because they didn't recognize the financial institution. After seeking advice from an attorney, Ryan and Clarice were able to successfully challenge the bank by proving they were victims of identity theft. But it ended up costing them a lot of time and money to resolve a situation that could have been avoided if they had taken immediate action when they received the first letter from the bank.

Following are some steps to take if you're the victim of identity theft.

Notify your creditors and banks right away. The longer you wait to contact these financial institutions, the higher your liability for the unauthorized charges. Document every conversation you have with the creditor or bank representative. Note the name of the person you speak with and the date and time of your call. You can use the Identity Theft Correspondence Worksheet located at the end of this chapter to help you track your conversations.

Your liability for unauthorized charges varies. Under the Electronic Fund Transfer Act, your liability for debit card fraud depends on when you report it. If you report the debit card lost or stolen within two business days, you're liable for up to $50 of any unauthorized charges. If you report *after* two business days but within sixty days after you noticed the unauthorized charges, you may be liable for up to $500. After sixty days, if you still have not reported the debit card lost or stolen, you could lose all the money that was withdrawn from your account. However, Visa and MasterCard will limit your liability for unauthorized use of your debit card, if it carries the Visa or MasterCard logo, in most cases to $50 per card regardless of how much time passed since you realized your card was lost or stolen.

The Fair Credit Billing Act limits your liability for unauthorized charges on your credit card to $50. If you discover that someone has stolen your checks, contact your bank immediately. You can find out information about your state laws regarding counterfeit checks by contacting your state banking department.

Create a fraud alert on your credit report. In addition to notifying your creditors and banks, you must also contact the credit reporting agencies to place a fraud alert on your file. Once you create a fraud alert, an identity thief will not be able to open new credit in your name. To establish a fraud alert, contact one of the three credit reporting agencies, and they'll notify the two others once you create the alert.

    Equifax: 800-525-6285, <www.equifax.com>
    Experian: 888-397-3742, <www.experian.com>
    TransUnion: 800-680-7289, <www.transunion.com>

There are two types of fraud alerts: an initial alert and an extended alert. An initial alert will remain on your file for ninety days and entitles you to one free credit report from each of the three credit reporting agencies. The initial alert is most commonly used when you believe you've been a victim of identity theft or if your wallet was lost or stolen. An extended alert will stay on your file for seven years and entitles you to two free credit reports within the year from each of the credit reporting agencies.

Contact the Social Security Administration. If your Social Security card was lost or stolen, you need to notify Social Security. In some cases you'll be issued a new Social Security number. However, if you've filed for bankruptcy, or if there's no evidence that your card is lost or stolen, you won't be able to get a new Social Security number. Instead, request a replacement card. Contact the Social Security Administration at <www.socialsecurity.gov> or 800-772-1213.

If your driver's license was stolen, contact the state agency that issued the license. You'll be given instructions on how to cancel your license and order a replacement.

File a police report. Some creditors require proof of identity theft, which can be accomplished with a police report. Be persistent in filing the report, as some police departments are reluctant to make it. If this situation occurs, request that the police file a "Miscellaneous Incidents" report. You can also contact your state attorney general's office to find out if the law in your state requires the police to make an identity theft report. Once you have the report, keep a copy in your records. You may need it in the future if problems arise that are associated with the identity theft.

Contact your local postal inspector. If you suspect that a thief has used a Change of Address form to forward your mail to another location, notify the postal inspector of the situation. Postal inspectors are given the duty of protecting the United States mail system from criminal misuse. You can find your local postal inspector by calling 877-876-2455 or visiting <http://postalinspectors.uspis.gov>.

Check your credit report often. It's crucial to continue checking your credit report after being victimized by identity theft. Order your credit report from all three credit reporting agencies, and make sure to review each entry for accuracy. Review the dates, amounts, and account numbers to determine if the entry is correctly reported. If you find an entry that's fraudulent or inaccurate, dispute it. The following chapter has information on how to handle credit disputes.

File a complaint with the Federal Trade Commission (FTC). This federal agency has the capability to forward complaints to the appropriate government agencies and companies for further investigation and action. You can contact the FTC by calling 877-IDTHEFT (438-4338) or visiting <www.consumer.gov/idtheft>.

TOUGH-TIME TIPS

- The most important thing you can do to prevent identity theft or deal with the aftermath is to be proactive.
- If you've been the victim of identity theft, keep a copy of all documents and papers associated with the theft, and hold on to any originals.

Example

Identity Theft Correspondence Worksheet

Use this form to keep track of your correspondence with the banks and creditors you contact

Date	Company	Contact	Conversation	Follow-up Letter Sent?
3/15/XX	EZ Credit	Jane Doe	Jane with EZ Credit has notated the fraud and will close the account.	Yes. I sent letter on 3/16/XX

PROTECT YOURSELF FROM IDENTITY THEFT

Identity Theft Correspondence Worksheet

Use this form to keep track of your correspondence with the banks and creditors you contact

Date	Company	Contact	Conversation	Follow-up Letter Sent?

My Financial Institutions

Use this form to keep track of all the credit card and bank accounts you currently have. Keep this form in a safe place.

Creditor _____

Address _____

Telephone Number _____

Credit Card/Account Number _____

Creditor _____

Address _____

Telephone Number _____

Credit Card/Account Number _____

Creditor _____

Address _____

Telephone Number _____

Credit Card/Account Number _____

Creditor _____

Address _____

Telephone Number _____

Credit Card/Account Number _____

Creditor _____

Address _____

Telephone Number _____

Credit Card/Account Number _____

16
BUILD YOUR CREDIT REPORT

Let your light shine before men, that they may see your
good deeds and praise your Father in heaven.
—Matthew 5:16

Once you've climbed your way out of the financial hole, it's important to ensure that your credit report is accurate and your credit score reflects your efforts. God has never left you, even when you felt you were alone. He will be faithful to help you rebuild your life and finances. This chapter contains some pointers to help you do your part.

A good credit report with a high credit scores is important in today's culture. If your credit report has been tarnished, there are ways to improve it.

CREDIT REPORTING AGENCIES

Three major credit reporting agencies serve the United States: Experian, TransUnion, and Equifax. The subscribers are the creditors who report information and your payment history to the reporting agencies. These subscribers do not report to all the credit reporting agencies unless they're paying members. That's why an individual may have an item on one credit report that does not appear on another. Both positive and negative accounts show up on the credit reports.

There's a limit to how long certain items remain on credit reporting agency files.

Bankruptcies must be removed after ten years.

Judgments, paid tax liens, and most other unfavorable information such as slow pays, charge-offs, repossessions, or delinquent accounts must be removed after seven years.

Unpaid tax liens will remain on your report until paid.

We recommend when applying for a car, home loan, or any type of credit that you request a copy of your credit report from all three of the reporting agencies to make sure there are no errors or inaccuracies showing up. It's also important to check your credit scores.

If you've applied for credit and your application has been denied, the creditor must send you a letter within thirty days stating

BUILD YOUR CREDIT REPORT

the reason credit was denied. If you were denied, you're entitled to a free credit report from the credit reporting agency listed in the denial letter. You must request a copy of the credit report within sixty days of the denial letter. A copy of the denial letter should be included with your request. If the denial letter is not available, mention the name of the company that refused you credit in your letter to the credit reporting agency.

It's a good idea to request copies of your credit report from Experian, Equifax, and TransUnion at least once a year to make sure the information is correct. You're entitled to receive a free annual credit report from all three credit reporting companies. You can request your annual credit report at <www.annualcreditreport.com>.

When requesting a copy of your credit report, a husband and wife must request their credit reports separately. If you were not turned down for credit and have already received your annual credit report for the year, you must send a fee for each additional report. Each state has different fees. Contact each credit reporting agency to see what the fee is.

After receiving a copy of your report, check each entry for accuracy. If inaccurate information appears on your credit report, that must be corrected before you apply for credit.

Credit reports can be ordered online. If you order online, be prepared to answer a question regarding one of your active accounts. For example, what is the payment for your GMAX account? (A) $200 (B) $300 (C) $400 (D) $450. If you answer wrong, they won't release the report.

If you request your credit reports by mail from TransUnion, Equifax, and Experian, include your full name, address, previous address, Social Security number, and date of birth. Include a copy of your driver's license or some type of billing statement with your name and address printed on it. This is for identification purposes. Also include the necessary fee if required.

Credit reporting agencies contact information

Free annual credit report: 877-322-8228 or <www.annualcreditreport.com>
TransUnion: 800-888-4213, <www.tuc.com>
Equifax: 800-685-1111, <www.equifax.com>
Experian: 888-397-3742, <www.experian.com>

After receiving a copy of your credit report, determine the status of your credit file. You should attempt to remove all inaccurate, incorrect, incomplete, and erroneous information shown.

If you've found errors in your credit report, you can dispute the inaccuracies or errors on the credit reporting agency's web site. You can also write to the credit bureau disputing the entries you feel are inaccurately reported. Don't put more than four items you are disputing in one letter. Study each entry to see if the item indicates the correct status. Are the dates correct? The amounts correct? Account numbers correct? Study each entry carefully to see what's inaccurate. If it's indeed inaccurate, you may file a dispute. If you choose to mail your dispute, mail the dispute letter by regular mail. Whichever way you dispute the item, via mail or web site, you can expect an updated report between forty-five to sixty days from the date you sent your dispute. The corrections and deletions should be reflected on the updated report. If there are more than four items you wish to dispute, mail a separate letter thirty days after the first letter was sent, listing the additional items.

When a dispute is filed with the credit bureau, it's the creditor's responsibility to respond to the credit bureau's inquiry about the disputed item. If the dispute is not answered by the creditor within a reasonable time, by federal law the item must be removed. This will result in the item being deleted from the credit bureau's files. The investigation with the creditors must be completed within thirty days of receipt of your letter or dispute. If you wish to repeat this procedure on any items that were not deleted or corrected, wait 120 days from the date of the last updated report to mail new letters.

If the creditor doesn't respond within that time period, the credit reporting agency must remove from the credit report the entry you're disputing. If the creditor does respond and corrects the inaccurate entry, the credit reporting agency will update your credit report. There is also the possibility that the creditor may respond and not make any changes to the credit report.

It's important that you dispute your inaccurate information with all three credit reporting agencies. If an item comes off one credit bureau report, there's no guarantee it will come off the other two. Remember: each credit reporting agency gets its information from its paid subscribers who are the creditors reporting the information. Don't make up an untrue story. Don't try to change your identity, and don't dispute information that's accurate. If you're mailing your letters, handwrite them or use your letterhead. This will add a personal touch to the letter. You can also use the dispute form that the credit reporting agency includes with your credit report. (See sample letters.)

You can also contact the creditor directly to see if they'll remove or correct the inaccurate information from your report. If the creditor agrees to this, ask them to send you a letter. Check your credit reports six weeks later to make sure the creditor followed through with the correction. If the creditor failed to follow through, send to the credit reporting agency a copy of the letter you received from the creditor. This will usually help get the correction made.

If you're not satisfied with the results, add a 100-word statement to the credit report indicating your side of the story.

CREDIT REPORTING ACTS

Being familiar with the Fair Credit Reporting Act and the Fair Accurate Credit Transaction Act—known as the FACT Act or FACTA—will help you when you dispute inaccurate information on your credit report. It will help you know what your legal rights are.

The FACT Act is the newest law that also contains provisions to help reduce identity theft.

You can request a free copy of the Fair Credit Reporting Act and the Fair and Accurate Credit Transactions Act from the Federal Trade Commission at <www.ftc.gov>.

CHEX SYSTEMS

If you've had a bank account closed for any reason, such as non-sufficient funds or overdrafts, and you never paid any money you owed to the bank, your name may appear on a reporting system called Chex Systems.

Many banks subscribe to Chex Systems. If your name appears on the Chex Systems report and you try to open a checking or savings account your request may be denied.

Chex Systems is regulated by the Fair Credit Reporting Act. You can dispute the entry the same way you would a credit report. Ask the bank who has denied you to give you the name of the bank that issued the negative report. Also ask for the address of Chex Systems to receive a copy of your Chex Systems report.

Sample Credit Report Request Form

Following is a sample letter to help you write your own letter within sixty days of having been denied credit.

SAMPLE ONLY—DO NOT USE.

Dear [name of credit agency]:

Please send me a free copy of my credit report. I was turned down for credit by [name of creditor that denied credit].

Full name: _____

Current address: _____

City _____ State _____ ZIP _____

Previous address _____

City _____ State _____ ZIP _____

BUILD YOUR CREDIT REPORT

Social Security number: _____

Date of birth: _____

Sincerely,

[Sign your name]

[Enclose a copy of your driver's license and any bill with your name and address printed on it for identification.]

Sample Credit Report Request Form

Following is a sample letter to help you write your own letter if you have not been turned down for credit.

SAMPLE ONLY—DO NOT USE.

Dear [name of agency],

Please send me a copy of my credit report. I am enclosing the necessary fee.

Full name: _____

Current address: _____

City _____ State _____ ZIP _____

Previous address _____

City _____ State _____ ZIP _____

Social Security number: _____

Date of birth: _____

Sincerely,

[Sign your name]

[Enclose a copy of your driver's license and any bill with your name and address printed on it for identification.]

Sample Dispute Letter #1

[Date]

Dear Credit Bureau:

I am responding to the credit report I received from your company. Following is a list of the errors contained in that report.

1. I have never paid Nelson Company thirty days late, account number 12340. Please correct this.

2. My account at ABC Company was paid in full and not charged off. Please remove this.

3. I do not owe this tax lien, docket #2222222.

4. Company Collection account #4444444 is not mine.

My name is Joe L. Smith, and I live at 4322 Park Ave., Anytown, CA 77777. My Social Security number is 222-00-0000. My previous address was 8765 Spring Parkway, Anytown, CA 77777. My date of birth is 11/07/1965.

Sincerely,

Joe L. Smith

Sample Dispute Letter #2

Send this letter thirty days after sending Letter #1.

[Date]

Dear Credit Bureau:

I am responding to a credit report I received from your company. Following is a list of errors contained in that report.

1. This bankruptcy docket #987768 for $125,000, dated 9-21-98,

is wrong and should not be on my credit report. Please remove this.

2. My account at Websters Company was paid off in full and was not a collection account. Please remove this.

3. Auto Mart, account number 290596, was paid as agreed and should have a positive rating. Please correct this.

My name is Joe L. Smith, and I live at 4322 Park Ave., Anytown, CA 77777. My Social Security number is 222-00-0000. My previous address was 8765 Spring Parkway, Anytown, CA 77777. My date of birth is 11/07/1965.

Sincerely,

Joe L. Smith

Questionnaire

From the list below, select the appropriate statements regarding each account. This will assist you in writing your letters.

Creditors

_____

_____

_____

_____

1. This is not my account.
2. This was not late as indicated.
3. This was not charged off.
4. This was paid in full as agreed.
5. This was not a collection account.
6. This is not my bankruptcy as indicated.
7. This is not my tax lien as indicated.

8. This is not my judgment as indicated.

Tracking Dispute Letters

Track the dates you sent dispute letters to the credit bureau. Indicate when you received your updated credit report and results.

Date   Bureau   Dispute   Update rec'd   Removed   Corrected

_____

_____

_____

_____

_____

_____

_____

Credit Scores

Your credit score, also known as your FICO score, is a three-digit number representing your creditworthiness as determined by credit reports. Each of the three credit reporting agencies has a slightly different formula for calculating scores, but all three are developed by FICO. Scores range from 300 to 850. Lenders use the scores from the credit reporting agencies as estimates of their potential risk in issuing the loan. The higher the number, the higher the likelihood the borrower will repay the loan. Scoring that uses a different set of parameters is also done for insurance companies and other businesses.

Lenders review a variety of information sources to aid them in the approval process. They will review at least one, and maybe more, of the applicant's credit reports.

Five major categories comprise your credit score. Following is a description of each category and the weight it carries in determining a consumer's score.

PAYMENT HISTORY
THIRTY-FIVE PERCENT

Payment history is a huge factor in your score. Lenders want to know your track record in repaying other loans. Late payments are not a complete negative; however, they are definitely frowned upon. An overall good credit score can outweigh one or two late payments. It's also important to realize that having no late payments does not guarantee automatic approval.

AMOUNT OF OUTSTANDING DEBT
THIRTY PERCENT

Many consumers carry balances on their credit cards, car loans, mortgages, and other types of accounts. Depending on the amounts owed, outstanding debt can mean the consumer is overextended, which may lead to late payments or loan default. This is a determining factor in whether or not the applicant can manage more credit.

Lowering your credit limits will hurt your credit score. The credit score is based on the debt utilization ratio—the total debt as a percentage of all your available credit. To improve your credit score, don't reduce your available credit. Rather, pay down your debt as quickly as possible. People with a debt utilization score of ten to twenty percent receive the best credit scores as long as they make their payments on time.

One of the big causes of a low credit score is high balances compared to the credit limit. Keep your balances below thirty percent of the credit limit.

LENGTH OF CREDIT HISTORY
FIFTEEN PERCENT

A longer, positive credit history increases your score. However, shorter credit histories may still receive high credit scores depending on other factors.

Closing an older credit card can cause your credit score to go down for a couple of reasons. First, the best scores go to people who use credit moderately over a long period of time. If you need to close some accounts, close the newest ones, so the cards with the longest history of on-time payments remain open. If you reduce your available credit by closing your credit cards, your utilization rate will look higher, thus lowering your score.

If you don't have a credit history, it will be hard to get a major loan. No credit is as bad as a negative credit report.

NEW CREDIT
TEN PERCENT

Opening several new accounts or having too many inquiries into your credit history in a short period of time can negatively affect your chances of qualifying for credit. However, the FICO scoring system distinguishes between opening several new credit accounts and shopping around for cards that carry lower interest rates, so it doesn't hurt to shop for competitive rates.

For example, if you're shopping for a mortgage, and several mortgage companies pull your credit report, the credit scoring agencies lump these inquiries into one inquiry. The window for this is a two-week period. Don't drag your comparison shopping out for too long, or the excessive inquiries will hurt your score.

If you request a copy of your credit report for yourself from any one of the three credit reporting agencies, this is a "soft" inquiry and does not impact your score.

TYPES OF CREDIT USED
TEN PERCENT

Types of credit used is usually not a major factor in the lender's decision to extend credit; however, if there is not much information in the other categories, types of credit used becomes more important. This takes into consideration the mix of credit cards, loans, finance accounts, and mortgages you have.

***

These categories are all considered in determining your credit score. Depending on the information in your credit report, one factor can play a more important role in your overall score regardless of the percentage any particular factor contributes.

CREDIT SCORE TIPS

- Negative entries decrease your score.
- Public notices such as bankruptcies, judgments, and tax liens hurt your score.
- If your balances are high compared to your credit limit, your score goes down.
- Low balances on your accounts increase your score.
- Limit your lines of credit to three or four credit cards.
- The older the account, the higher the score.
- Borrowing from finance companies lowers your score.
- Excessive inquiries lower your score.

FICO CREDIT SCORING

Below 585: Very High Risk. May not qualify for loan or credit.
585—619: High Risk. May not qualify for the best rates.
620—679: Lender may take a closer look at credit report.
680—718: Good Credit.
Above 719: Excellent Credit

Since FICO scores are used frequently in qualifying for credit, it's recommended that you keep two or three lines of credit open and close everything else. If you have no credit activity, your FICO score can be low. One way to get good FICO scores is to charge small purchases. For example, charge $25 per month, and pay it off each month. This will reflect a good payment pattern.

A new scoring system, VantageScore, may be introduced in the future. Most of the lending institutions continue to use the Fair Isaac model.

According to the credit reporting agencies, VantageScore uses a numeric scale of 501 to 990 and also a parallel alphabetic scale that classifies consumers into fixed A, B, C, D, or F scoring. It's hard to judge if and when the lenders will embrace this new type of scoring.

Always be aware of ways to maintain or improve your score. Don't get carried away and begin running up your debt again. Remember how hard it was to pay your high debt off?

TOUGH-TIME TIPS

- Get a copy of your credit report from all three credit reporting agencies to make sure there are no errors.
- Get a copy of your credit report from each reporting agency at least once a year or prior to making a major purchase such as a home or automobile. Request your FICO score.
- Don't close all unused credit cards.
- Dispute inaccurate entries on your credit report to the credit reporting agency reporting the item.
- Keep the balances on your credit cards below thirty percent of the credit limit.

17

MONEY MIRACLES

Encourage one another daily,
as long as it is called Today.
—Hebrews 3:13

MONEY TROUBLE

As we put our trust in the Lord, He's faithful to walk with us through our trials. These blessings come in many forms. Financial trials are definitely times we need God's help, and He's waiting to lead us. He cares about all aspects of our lives, including our finances.

Jesus reminds us that God watches over us:

> I tell you, do not worry about your life, what you will eat or drink; or about your body, what you will wear. Is not life more important than food, and the body more important than clothes? Look at the birds of the air; they do not sow or reap or store away in barns, and yet your heavenly Father feeds them. Are you not much more valuable than they? Who of you by worrying can add a single hour to his life? (Matthew 6:25-27).

Over the years we've seen God's hand in our own lives and in the lives of others. We believe you'll be encouraged and motivated by these stories and will be led to examine your own life to discover all that God has done for you.

A Christmas to Remember

Deborah

Many years ago when my three daughters were in elementary school, we faced financial challenges. It was Christmas time, and I began to think of what I had been thankful for during that year. One of those things was the health of my family. With the turbulent previous years and constant health problems with my children and family, I really was thankful for that. I began to think about what I could do to help someone else in need.

I contacted our county hospital and asked if there were any children who would be in the hospital for Christmas. The caseworker said there were eight terminally ill children who would be spending Christmas in the hospital. She told me their ages and genders, and she also indicated the family of one of the children was in great financial need.

I had only $100 to work with. It became a family project, and the goal was to get the presents and deliver them before Christmas Eve.

My three daughters and I watched and searched the newspaper for sales as we began the shopping. My daughters became so excited that they came to my husband and me. "Mom and Dad, don't buy us Christmas presents this year. Use the money to buy more presents for these needy children."

After our shopping was done, the whole family spent the evening wrapping the gifts for the children in the hospital. We also bought a gift certificate for food for the family in need. I don't know how we did it, but the $100 went a long way, and each child received more than one gift.

My husband, Hal, and the girls put the presents in a large, green trash bag, and Hal slung the bag over his shoulder like Santa Clause, and off we went to deliver the presents.

On Christmas Day as Tiffany, Christy, and Melinda opened their own gifts, they stopped several times to wonder out loud how the children at the hospital were enjoying their gifts. It was a Christmas we will all remember, and a blessing for each of us.

The blessing didn't stop that day, however. Two weeks after Christmas, we received an unexpected check for $100 in the mail due to an overpayment on an insurance policy!

God Had a Plan

Melinda

I've experienced many miracles throughout my life, including some involving money. When we struggled financially with career changes and moves, God always provided for us.

Mike and I had regularly donated to a local charity to sponsor children who wanted to attend church camp but didn't have the means to pay their own way. These children came from broken homes, and many of them had experienced violence.

One year I didn't know how we were going to afford the donation to send a child to camp. Money was very tight for us that summer, and I just didn't think we could do it. However, I still felt that God was putting it in my heart to give, even though it would create a financial strain. As I struggled with the decision of whether or not to give, I received a check in the mail for a reimbursement from an account that I had overpaid. The amount of the check was almost exactly what was needed to sponsor a child. When I received that check, I knew exactly what it was to be used for, and we were able to make our donation. My husband and I also felt wonderfully blessed.

Stepping Out in Faith

Julie

My husband and I had just paid off our credit card debt, and were committed to living within our means. We had also made a commitment to tithe to our church.

We had some unexpected expenses that month—a broken dishwasher, doctor appointments, and unpaid time off work because of sick children. Our expenses for the month were more than our income.

I questioned whether or not we should give our tithe to the church, because we were not going to have enough for the mortgage payment. I sat in church and prayed and decided to write the check for the tithe.

The next day we received an $800 check in the mail from the escrow account with our lender, which covered our mortgage payment for the month.

Just Ask

Stacie

I know that God answers prayer. He continually provides for my needs and my family's.

A few years ago while we were living in San Antonio, I began having migraine headaches. The doctor told me that the headaches were caused by allergies. During the time we lived there, I also got inner-ear infections, sinus infections, and allergy-related mononucleosis. The illnesses finally stopped once we moved away.

My husband, Mark, began attending seminary, and we worked at the seminary and lived in seminary housing while he finished his degree. Our jobs did not pay well, and money was tight. The house we lived in was more than 100 years old, and the neighborhood was unsafe; it was not uncommon to hear gunfire at night.

Eventually we moved to Roanoke, Texas, and got new jobs. One morning when I was getting ready for work, I passed out in the shower. I went to work that day, but at the office I called my doctor, who immediately scheduled an MRI. That night I received a phone call informing me that I had a brain tumor.

Following that diagnosis, I was unable to work because of the medical treatments. Although my husband and I looked for ways I could make extra money to help with the bills, money just seemed to get tighter.

A friend of Mark's called Mark several times to tell him about a great job opportunity. At the time, Mark was happy at his job and wasn't really looking for a new one. He finally decided to go for an interview, and he was hired. His salary increased forty-two percent. Plus, his new employer allows him to accompany me to my medical appointments.

We've consistently felt God's hand on our lives. He has not left me and my family in need. We're walking testimonies that God always provides. All you have to do is ask.

God Always Gives Me What I Need

Karen

It was my first holiday season as the single mother of Jason, 10, and Lori, 8. After paying the mortgage on our three-bedroom home, as well as utilities and food expenses, I had no money left for presents. I felt anxious and sad, knowing I would not be able to provide the children with the kind of holiday they had always had. Exactly one week before Christmas, I received a check in the mail from my mortgage company for $350. It seems I had overpaid my escrow account that year and was being refunded the difference.

There have been other times since then that I've seen God's hand in my finances. I've come to believe that I don't always get what I want—but with faith I always get what I need.

Unexpected Hailstorm

Tracey

I had lost seventy-five percent of my income, and my husband and I were struggling financially. Our car was falling apart—and probably on its last leg. We were afraid it would break down, and we didn't have money for any repairs. We prayed to God that the car would keep running. Who would have thought that the money we needed would be provided by a hailstorm? That hailstorm dented my old car, and I was able to recover $6,000 by filing a claim with my insurance company. We were able to replace my old car with the $6,000 we received because of hail damage.

Witnesses of God's Faithfulness and Protection

Molly

My husband, Jimmy, and I are personal witnesses of God's faithfulness and protection. Jimmy was a youth pastor for nine years, and we loved working in youth ministry. However, it was difficult to raise our family on Jimmy's salary. Whenever a new senior pastor was hired at the church, most of the other ministry positions were also replaced, so we frequently changed churches. Every eighteen months or so, we were looking for another youth pastor position, and sometimes it took several months to find something.

One year we attended a church retreat. While we were there, someone told us that we would be blessed financially. Both of us knew that God was true to His word, but it was difficult to imagine that our finances would be taken care of.

Then we moved to a place where we were both able to find jobs. Things were looking up, and we saved and bought our first house. Seven months later, we were forced to change churches again, and we relocated to another city.

We put our house on the market, but it didn't sell. Jimmy

started working at the new church, and we found a home to rent. However, we were making a mortgage payment plus paying rent. On paper we were $1,000 short every month. I fretted, because I knew we couldn't make ends meet. But God took care of us. Every month for one full year we received an unexpected check, gift, or refund that equaled $1,000. One month it was a gift from the Sunday School, and another month it was a tax rebate we weren't expecting. There was even a flood that totaled our car! The insurance company paid for the car, and we got an additional $1,000. After a few months of this, I started to laugh and said, "Okay, Lord—I'll never doubt you again." From that point, things got better.

Our financial needs were met each and every month. At the end of the twelve months, we rented out our house, and the rent paid our mortgage for the upcoming year. Eventually we changed jobs again and moved back to our home. We didn't have work lined up, but we trusted in God and felt peace.

As we were moving back in August, one of Jimmy's friends mentioned that Jimmy should consider working for the market research company where the friend worked. His friend had also been in ministry, and he knew the financial instability that sometimes accompanied that line of work. After four months and much prayer, Jimmy took the job, feeling that the Lord was going to bless him so he could bless other ministers.

The job was a entry-level position at low pay, but we felt it was the right decision. Within three months, Jimmy was promoted and went on to win a sales award. Today he earns four times what he used to make. Every time he received a commission check, we send money to a youth pastor. Looking back, we can see that the events in our lives were orchestrated by God. We'll never doubt His provision.

*** * * ***

We hope you were blessed by these stories. We tell them to encourage you that God will provide. E-mail us at www.financialvictory.com to tell us your story of seeing God's hand in your finances.

18
FINANCIAL VICTORY

This is the day the Lord has made;
let us rejoice and be glad in it.
—Psalm 118:24

With your newfound financial freedom, you can rejoice and begin setting new financial goals. Your first goal should be to build wealth rather than debt. By building wealth, you'll be able to tithe more to your church and give more to charities, as well as live your life in financial victory.

Don't look back. You learn through mistakes, but God wants you to stay focused on the new things ahead and to keep moving forward. With God as your partner, you won't slip back.

After all you've been through, you should reward yourself! Just be sure you do it in a way that will keep you moving forward.

A NEW YOU!

With financial freedom comes a new set of financial goals. Your first goal was to find a solution to your financial problem and to work your way out of debt.

Your new goal should be to build your new financial future. The most important thing you can do is to break your old spending habits. If you don't, you may be tempted to start misusing credit cards again and mismanaging your finances.

There will be days that you feel the urge to go and spend. That's normal. But don't do it! If you find yourself in a situation that tempts you to make an impulsive purchase with your credit card—or to open a new account—leave the store. Go home and sleep on it. As stated before, usually that urge will be gone by the next day, and you will have saved yourself from falling into the debt cycle again.

If you refinanced your home or took out an equity loan on your home to pay off your debt, don't start using your credit cards, and don't tap into your equity line of credit. If you do, you run the risk of running up more debt, your debt ratio will be too high, and you stand the chance of going bankrupt or losing your home in foreclosure.

Plan ahead what you'll spend on a weekly, monthly, and yearly basis. Have regular meetings with your spouse so you both agree on all the expenditures.

You can begin saving once you've broken the habits of spending too much and carrying too much debt. By getting into the habit of applying the extra money you're saving from paying off debt, you can begin saving and giving more to your church and charities. All the money you were using to pay off your debts can begin to work for you and others in need instead of against you. You can begin to save more money by making wise choices.

Goals

1. Start saving your money. Try to save at least ten percent of your take-home pay. Contact a financial planner to help you invest your money so that it will be safe and will grow.

2. Use at least ten percent of your income for tithing. Give to your local charity, church, or religious organization, or any needy cause. It feels great to know you're helping others.

3. Don't use credit cards for purchases unless you have the money to pay the bill in full when it arrives. Follow your budget. Pay by check or debit card, and register each purchase. Open a checking account that pays interest. Keep a spending journal with you to allocate how your cash is spent and what you charged. This will remind you not to make frivolous purchases.

4. Open a separate account to deposit money for your non-monthly expenses such as property taxes, insurance, auto maintenance, repairs, and so on. Make deposits into this account every month based on your yearly budget.

5. Save up an emergency fund that equals at least four months living expenses.

6. Set up a retirement account. Social Security won't be enough for you to live on. Open an IRA or 401K. Your

employer may match part of your contribution, making your investment worth even more.
7. Buy insurance to protect your family. Shop around and buy only what you need.
8. Consult a financial planner to determine how much you should save each month to apply toward retirement.
9. Purchase a home. By doing so, you have the security of an investment that will increase in value. You can also write off your interest and property taxes.
10. Establish college funds. More and more students are going to college. If you're able to set aside money toward your child's education, you'll eliminate either you or your child having to take out student loans. The earlier you start saving, the more you'll have. Financial planners can help you calculate the cost of college and how much you should be saving on a monthly basis.

FINAL NOTE

Our prayer for you is found in 3 John 2—"Beloved, I pray that you may prosper in all things and be in health, just as your soul prospers" (NKJV).

TOUGH-TIME TIPS

- Pay God first.
- If you feel the urge to make an impulsive purchase, go home and sleep on it.
- Don't run up new charges after you've refinanced your home or tapped into your equity line of credit to pay off your bills—not even "just this once."
- Have three to six months of living expenses saved as an emergency fund.

MAKING DREAMS COME TRUE

Now that you have your finances under control and can

breathe, make a list of dreams you can turn into reality, and go for it. List all the things you can now do as a result of financial victory. Here are some examples to get your dream list started.

Give more to your place of worship and charities.

Start your own business.

Take a vacation.

Save for your dream home.

Invest for retirement.

Start a college fund.

A Personal Pledge

- If I'm tempted to use my credit cards, I'll walk away from the situation and sleep on the purchase.
- I'll pay off my credit card balances every month.
- I'll keep a daily journal of all my expenses, credit card charges, and cash expenditures.
- I'll tithe at least ten percent of my income.
- I'll put at least ten percent of my income into a savings plan.
- I'll have monthly meetings with my spouse to review our budget.
- I'll set financial goals.
- I'll pay the mortgage, rent, utilities, and food bills first.
- I'll seek help from a credit counselor or financial adviser if my debt ratio exceeds twenty percent of my income or if I'm having trouble paying my bills.
- I'll seek the assistance of a financial planner to make a plan for retirement and investments.
- I'll take God as my partner and continually pray for wisdom, strength, and peace.

Signature _____ Date _____

Spouse's signature _____ Date _____

We would love to hear about your financial victories.

If you have questions or would like to book a media interview or speaking engagement, contact Financial Victory Institute.

Visit us at <http://financialvictory.com>,
or call our office at 888-838-4768.

ADDITIONAL RESOURCES

CREDIT COUNSELING/DEBT MANAGEMENT
Cambridge Credit Counseling: consolidate bills, lower interest rates, debt management. 800-208-5084 <www.cambridgecredit.org>

CREDIT REPORTING AGENCIES
Free report under the Fair and Accurate Credit Transaction Act: 877-322-8228, <www.annualcreditreport.com>

Equifax: 800-685-1111, <www.equifax.com>

Experian: 888-397-3742, <www.experian.com>

TransUnion: 800-888-4213, <www.transunion.com>

FICO SCORES
FAIR ISAAC: source for FICO score and tips on improving it. <www.myfico.com>

SUPPORT FOR COMPULSIVE SPENDERS
Debtors Anonymous: a support group focusing on recovering from compulsive spending.
800-421-2383, <www.debtorsanonymous.org>

MORTGAGE INFORMATION
HSH Associates: publisher of consumer loan information. <www.hsh.com>

Fannie Mae—provides mortgage guidelines. <www.fanniemae.com>

Freddie Mac—provides mortgage guidelines. <www.freddiemac.com>

FHA Loans
U.S. Department of Housing and Urban Development: <www.hud.gov>

Loan Modification Counseling—<www.legacymoney.com>

FINANCIAL WEBSITES

Bankrate.com—Provides tools and information to help consumers make financial decisions. <www.bankrate.com>

Cardweb.com—an online publisher of information pertaining to all types of payment cards. <www.cardweb.com>

Financial Victory Institute—financial resource guide, education, and financial counseling. <www.fnancialvictory.com>

INSURANCE

Insurance Information Institute—a directory of insurance organizations, carriers, agents, brokers, and news links. <www.iii.org>

Medicare—information on the government program. <www.medicare.gov>

Medicaid
Contact your state health department for information. <www.cms.hhs.gov>

COBRA—offers extended insurance coverage. <www.dol.gov>, or contact your Human Resources Department.

GOVERNMENT AGENCIES

U.S. Department of Housing & Urban Development (HUD)
Contact your local HUD office for more information. <www.hud.gov/localoffices.cfm>

Office of Child Support Enforcement
Contact your state child support office to inquire on reducing or receiving child support payments. <www.acf.hhs.gov/programs/cse>

Social Security Administration, Social Security Disability Insurance, and Supplemental Security Income
800-772-1213, <www.ssa.gov>

Workers' Compensation
Contact your state government office to find out about workers' compensation laws and programs.

Unemployment Benefits
<www.workforcesecurity.doleta.gov>
Contact your state unemployment office for laws and programs in your state.

ADDITIONAL RESOURCES

Federal Trade Commission
877-FTC-HELP (382-4357), <www.ftc.gov>

LAWS

Fair and Accurate Credit Transactions Act
877-FTC-HELP (382-4357)
<www.ftc.gov/bcp/menus/consumer/credit/rights.shtm>

Fair Credit Reporting Act
877-FTC-HELP (382-4357)
<www.ftc.gov/bcp/conline/pubs/credit/fcra.htm>

Fair Credit Billing Act
877-FTC-HELP (382-4357)
<www.ftc.gov/bcp/conline/pubs/credit/fcb.htm>

Credit Repair Organizations Act
877-FTC-HELP (382-4357)
<www.ftc.gov/os/statutes/croa/croa.htm>

Fair Debt Collection Practices Act
877-FTC-HELP (382-4357)
<www.ftc.gov/os/statutes/fdcpa/fdcpact.htm>

Equal Credit Opportunity Act
877-FTC-HELP (382-4357)
<www.ftc.gov/bcp/conline/pubs/credit/ecoa.htm>

Truth in Lending Act
877-275-ASK-FDIC (275-3342)
<www.fdic.gov/regulations/laws/rules/6500-1400.html>

ABOUT THE AUTHORS

Deborah McNaughton is a nationally recognized author, credit expert, and financial coach with more than twenty-five years of experience. She is cofounder of Financial Victory Institute. Deborah is also a licensed real estate broker and president of Legacy Financial Services, Inc., an organization specializing in mortgages and financial counseling. She is a monthly columnist for First for Women magazine, and has been interviewed on hundreds of television and radio programs including Janet Parshall's America, Moody Broadcasting, CNN, CNN-FN, Bloomberg Television, Good Day New York, Lifetime New Attitudes, and many others. She has been quoted as a credit expert in Wall Street Journal, New York Times, Today's Christian Woman, Woman's Day, Parade, Your Money, Success Opportunities, Working Woman, and Income Opportunities.

Melinda Weinstein is an author, financial expert, and cofounder of Financial Victory Institute. She has more than eleven years of experience in the mortgage industry with seven years of credit counseling experience. Melinda has been interviewed on several television and radio programs that include Your Life A to Z (KTVK Phoenix), Arizona Midday (NBC Phoenix), Sonoran Living Live (ABC 15, KNXV-TV Phoenix), Janet Parshall's America, The Cooper Lawrence Show, and is senior columnist for "Marketwatch" on Your Money with Chuck Jaffe radio show. She has been quoted as a credit expert in magazines that include Woman's World and First for Women. She received an MBA from Arizona State University.

THE PRINCIPLE-CENTERED FINANCIAL SERIES

Simple, proven solutions to help you master money management

MANAGING YOUR MONEY
MATT SCHOENFELD
ISBN: 978-0-8341-2387-8

LEARNING TO INVEST
MATT SCHOENFELD
ISBN: 978-0-8341-2389-2

LIVING DEBT FREE
MATT SCHOENFELD
ISBN: 978-0-8341-2388-5

Let Matt Schoenfeld show you sensible and effective ways to
- set up a successful money management system,
- shrink and eliminate debt,
- secure your financial future,
- and bless and serve others with what you have.

Available wherever books are sold

BEACON HILL PRESS
OF KANSAS CITY

Manage your net worth with new perspective.

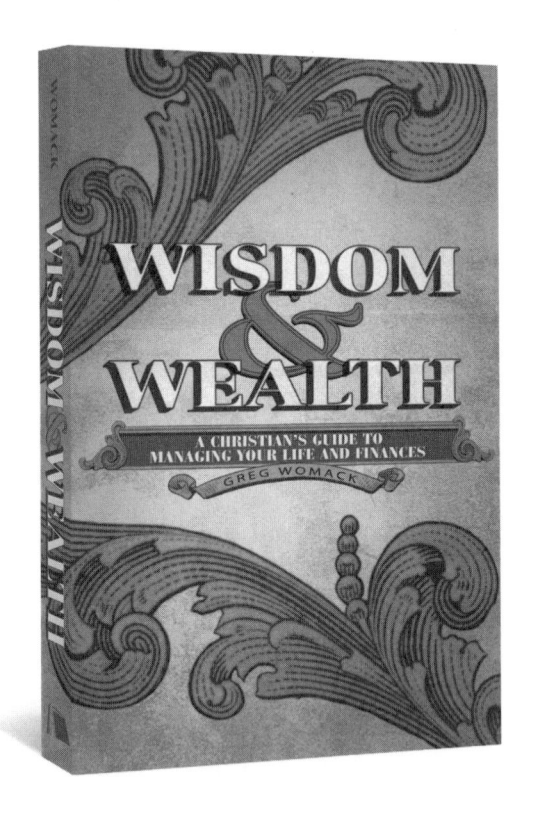

This beneficial resource will show you how to successfully manage your finances and learn to put your money where your faith is. Greg Womack, a certified financial planner, uses the time-tested wisdom of King Solomon to help you make wise financial choices, manage your money properly, and use what you have to bless and serve others.

WISDOM AND WEALTH
A Christian's Guide to Managing Your Life and Finances
Greg Womack
978-0-8341-2321-2

BEACON HILL PRESS
OF KANSAS CITY

www.beaconhillbooks.com